PONS

Typisch Englisch

von
Dr. Rebecca Davies

PONS GmbH
Stuttgart

PONS

TYPISCH ENGLISCH

von

Dr. Rebecca Davies

1. Auflage 2017

www.pons.de
E-Mail: info@pons.de

Redaktion: Dr. Birgit Reinel
Logoentwurf: Erwin Poell, Heidelberg
Logoüberarbeitung: Sabine Redlin, Ludwigsburg
Einbandgestaltung: Anne Helbich, Stuttgart
Titelfoto: Stiefel: Shutterstock/homydesign,
Pfeife: Shutterstock/ homydesign,
Tasse: Shutterstock/ M. Unal Ozmen,
Krone: Shutterstock/Robert Neal,
Rosen: iStockphoto/ Pazhyna
Layout: Petra Michel, Gestaltung & Typografie, Bamberg
Satz: tebitron gmbh, Gerlingen
Druck und Bindung: Multiprint GmbH

Printed in the EU.
ISBN: 978-3-12-562934-9

Very British!

Vertiefen Sie mit diesem Rätselbuch Ihr Wissen über Großbritannien und Irland und erweitern Sie Ihre Englisch-Kenntnisse in 20 großen Quiz-Themen. Dabei erfahren Sie noch mehr Interessantes, Unterhaltsames und Skurriles rund um die Inseln.

Die **20 Themen** stehen jeweils unter einem **Motto**, sei es eine Stadt, eine Region oder ein kulturelles Thema.
Dabei gibt es vier Rubriken, die farblich gekennzeichnet sind:

Mensch & Natur: ***Geschichte, Geographie, Politik, Wirtschaft etc.***

Kultur & Reisen: ***Kunst, Literatur, Sehenswürdigkeiten etc.***

Sprache & mehr: ***Sprache, Kommunikation, Humor, Rezepte etc.***

Rätseln & Knobeln: ***sprachliche und kulturelle Rätsel***

Inselhopping oder große Rundreise – das ist ganz Ihnen überlassen: Sie können sich entweder gezielt die Themen oder Rubriken aussuchen, die Sie am meisten interessieren oder aber Sie machen die ganze Reise rund um die Inseln.

Bei einigen Rätseln müssen Sie sicherlich ein wenig **raten** und **ausprobieren**, aber die ausführlichen **Lösungen** werden Ihnen helfen, Ihr Wissen über die Sprache, das Land und die Leute zu erweitern. Und wenn Sie einmal sprachlich nicht weiter wissen, hilft Ihnen das **Wortverzeichnis** zu den schwierigsten Wörtern.

Have a good trip!

Ihre Pons-Redaktion

Inhalt

Welcome to Britain! 6

Basic geography · British history · Top Ten Greatest Britons · British money · Hello and goodbye · Flags of the UK · National symbols

This sceptred isle 12

Invaders and conquerors · Stories of the sea · Dressing for the weather · Weather idioms · Arriving in Britain

London: a nation, not a city 16

London facts · Travelling on the Tube · Famous London sights · Visiting London · Who will you see where? · The East End · Cockney rhyming slang · Strange place names

Shop till you drop 22

Well-known chains · A nation of shopkeepers · Opening hours · Charity shops · Asking for help · In the department store · Buy British! · Companies

Westward Ho! 26

Sights of the South West · Which county is it? · Glastonbury fact file · Coastlines · Cornish pasties · Preparation method · Food and drink · Fact or fiction?

Always look on the bright side 32

Humour · Find the jokers · Comedy films · Jokes · Describing humour · Films and more · Restaurant jokes

It's grim up North – or is it? 36

Cities of the North · The industrial past · Actors and singers · Tourist attractions · Facts and figures · The North-South divide · Food specialities · Northern brands

Meet the royals 42

Historical periods · Politics and the monarchy · Official residences · Royal sightseeing · Royal ladies and gentlemen · The royal family · More royal names and titles

Scotland the Brave 46

Scotland's economy · Cities in Scotland · About Scotland · Tourist destinations · Inventive Scots · Scottish culture · Scottish words · Scotland fact file

This sporting life 52

British sport · History of sport · Sport in films · Rules of the game · Idioms from sport · Sport vocabulary · Disciplines

Wales – the Land of Song 56

Wales · Welsh slate · Welsh celebrities · Sightseeing in Wales · Facts about Wales · A Welsh snack · Welsh and German · Highest, longest, largest

On the roads and rails 62

Road signs · Vocabulary of driving · Rules of the road · Using public transport · Saving money · More public transport · Taxi!

Do you fancy a drink? 66

Tea break · Afternoon tea · The tea ceremony · Tea quiz · Pub culture · Pub snacks · Beer types · Drinks with little or no alcohol · Small talk at the pub

Glorious grub 72

British food brands · Eating internationally · Roast dinner · Traditional British dishes · False friends · Sandwich culture · English breakfast

Let's celebrate! 76

The fifth of November · Celebrations · Celebrating differently · Traditions and superstitions · Party small talk · Reasons to celebrate · Celebration customs · Wedding traditions

Politics and the news media 82

British politics · Elections and parliament · Prime ministers · More about British politics · Newspaper culture · Other news media · News and politics · British newspapers

Shakespeare's country 86

Birmingham · Other towns and cities · The Midlands · The industrial past and present · Robin Hood · Midlands specialities · Shakespeare's life and works · Shakespeare quotations

On screen: TV and film 92

British TV and film · History of the BBC · Murder mysteries and thrillers · British films · Film and TV vocabulary · Different genres · Bond, James Bond · British Oscar winners

The Emerald Isle 96

Ireland's main cities · The economy of Ireland · The Republic of Ireland · The road to peace · Places to visit · Famous Irish artists · Irish English · Guinness

Music and art in Britain 102

British bands · Music & Co. · Andrew Lloyd Webber · British composers · Tate Modern · British artists · Music and art

Anhang

Lösungen 106

Wortverzeichnis 117

Welcome to Britain!

Things to do on a trip to Britain

Welcome Erlebnisse dürfen bei keinem Großbritannienbesuch fehlen?

- ☐ ganz oben auf einem **double-decker bus** fahren
- ☐ sich nach einer Wanderung ein **real ale** in einem Pub gönnen
- ☐ in einem schönen Café oder Hotel einen **afternoon tea** zu sich nehmen
- ☐ sich über die riesige Auswahl an **Sandwich-Füllungen** freuen
- ☐ das bunte, **multikulturelle Leben** der Großstädte erkunden
- ☐ **fish & chips** am Strand bei einer Meeresbrise genießen
- ☐ sich mit den Spielregeln von **cricket, rugby** oder **snooker** befassen
- ☐ die Schönheit von **Wales** oder **Schottland** entdecken

Where are we?

Großbritannien ist die größte der so genannten **Britischen Inseln** und besteht aus **England, Schottland** und **Wales**. Zusammen mit **Nordirland** bilden diese vier Länder das **Vereinigte Königreich**. Im südlichen Teil der Nachbarinsel **Irland** befindet sich die **Republik Irland**.

Welcome to Britain!

Basic geography

Ordnen Sie zuerst die Länder den Zahlen auf der Karte zu. Verbinden Sie dann die Ländernamen mit den unten stehenden Oberbegriffen.

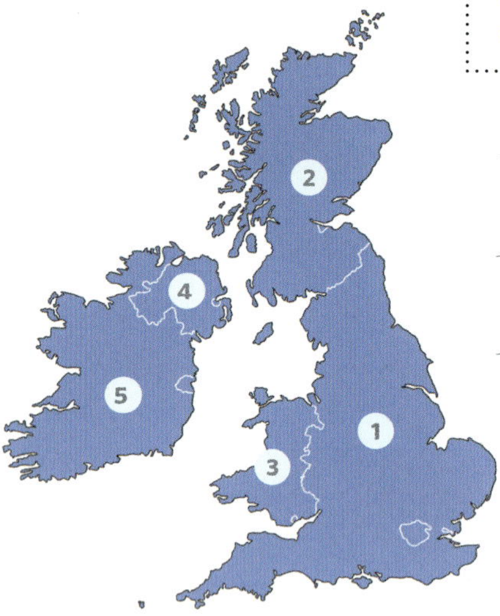

___ A Scotland

___ B Northern Ireland

___ C England

___ D Republic of Ireland

___ E Wales

Great Britain: ____________

United Kingdom: ____________

Ireland: ____________

British Isles: ____________

British history

In welchem Jahr fanden diese wichtigen Ereignisse in der Geschichte Großbritanniens und Irlands statt?

1. Teilung Irlands nach dem 1. Weltkrieg: Nordirland bleibt Teil des Vereinigten Königreichs, der Rest wird kurz darauf zur Irischen Republik.
2. Die vollständige politische Vereinigung von England, Wales und Schottland erfolgt ein Jahrhundert nach der Personalunion der Monarchien.
3. Großbritannien und Irland werden zum Vereinigten Königreich zusammengeführt, allerdings nur für 120 Jahre.
4. Jakob VI. von Schottland wird auch Jakob I. von England, kurz nach dem Tod Elisabeths I.
5. Als erster Schritt wird Wales in den Rechtsraum von England eingegliedert.

___ A 1536

___ B 1603

___ C 1707

___ D 1801

___ E 1921

Folgende Persönlichkeiten haben in einer BBC-Umfrage die Top Ten-Plätze der **100 Greatest Britons** belegt. Können Sie die Namen der richtigen Beschreibung zuordnen?

Top Ten Greatest Britons

Isambard Kingdom Brunel (1806–1859) war als Ingenieur für den Bau der **Great Western Railway** und des Themse-Tunnels verantwortlich. Mit der **Great Britain** baute er 1843 den weltweit ersten propellerbetriebenen Transatlantikdampfer.

1. Winston Churchill
2. Isambard Kingdom Brunel
3. Princess Diana
4. Charles Darwin
5. William Shakespeare
6. Isaac Newton
7. John Lennon
8. Queen Elizabeth I
9. Horatio Nelson
10. Oliver Cromwell

___ **A** engineer of ships, bridges, tunnels and more

___ **B** "Good Queen Bess", daughter of Henry VIII

___ **C** physicist and mathematician

___ **D** Puritan and political leader

___ **E** sea captain

___ **F** Beatles member

___ **G** evolution theorist

___ **H** prime minister, Nobel prize winner

___ **I** "Queen of Hearts", mother of Prince William

___ **J** England's national poet

Ordnen Sie die Münzen dem jeweils richtigen Geldwert zu.

British money

___ **A** 2p

___ **B** 50p

___ **C** 10p

___ **D** 1p

___ **E** £2

___ **F** 20p

___ **G** £1

___ **H** 5p

Welcome to Britain!

Hello and goodbye

Wie geht man am besten mit Gruß- und Abschiedsformeln um?

1. You arrive at a restaurant for dinner and would like to say something more formal than "Hello". Which is best?

- ☐ **A** Good morning.
- ☐ **B** Good night.
- ☐ **C** Good afternoon.
- ☐ **D** Good evening.

2. What do you say to someone you know but have not seen for a long time?

- ☐ **A** It's nice to meet you.
- ☐ **B** It's nice to see you again.
- ☐ **C** I hope to see you again soon.
- ☐ **D** Have a good journey.

3. A shop assistant says "Hello, can I help you?" to you. What can you say if you don't want to buy anything immediately?

- ☐ **A** No, you can't help.
- ☐ **B** Thank you, I'm just looking.
- ☐ **C** Can I see, please?
- ☐ **D** I want to look.

4. You are checking out of your hotel and want to thank the staff for their help: "Thank you for looking ... me."

- ☐ **A** for
- ☐ **B** around
- ☐ **C** after
- ☐ **D** at

5. You are finishing an enjoyable conversation with someone you have just met. What would you **not** say?

- ☐ **A** It was nice to meet you.
- ☐ **B** I enjoyed talking to you.
- ☐ **C** Thank you for the chat.
- ☐ **D** Thank you for the speech.

6. Which form is **not** used to end a business letter?

- ☐ **A** Lots of love,
- ☐ **B** Best wishes,
- ☐ **C** Kind regards,
- ☐ **D** Yours sincerely,

Nur beim allerersten Treffen geben sich die Briten üblicherweise die Hand und es ist unüblich, sich nur mit dem Nachnamen vorzustellen. In der Geschäftswelt stellt man sich meist mit Vor- und Nachnamen vor (**"Good morning. I'm Sarah Green."**). Im privatenUmgang wird heutzutage die Anrede mit Vornamen bevorzugt (**"Hi, Tom."**). Wert auf akademische Titel wird eigentlich nur im akademischen und medizinischen Bereich gelegt.

Flags of the UK

In den verschiedenen Regionen des Vereinigten Königreichs sind folgende Flaggen zu sehen. Ordnen Sie die Flaggen ihrem jeweiligen Geltungsgebiet zu.

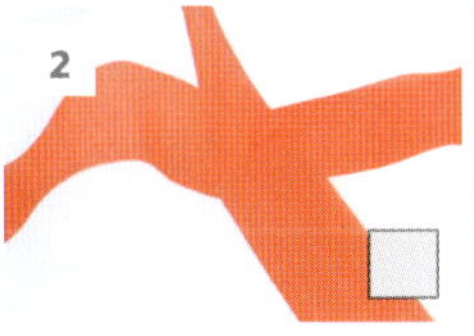

A The UK   **B** Wales   **C** Scotland   **D** England

National symbols

Die britische Flagge, genannt **Union Flag** oder **Union Jack,** wurde ursprünglich als Mischung aus den Flaggen Englands und Schottlands konzipiert; später kam dann noch eine irische Komponente hinzu. Wales ist nicht darauf repräsentiert, da es damals bereits zu England gehörte.

Bringen Sie die Buchstaben in die richtige Reihenfolge, um die englischen Begriffe für die hervorgehobenen Wörter zu finden.

1. Auf der walisischen Flagge ist ein **Drache** zu sehen.

   G A R N O D ____________

2. Schottlands Nationalblume ist die **Distel**.

   T E L I T H S ____________

3. Das **Einhorn** ist ebenfalls ein Symbol Schottlands.

   C U R N I N O ____________

4. Auf manchen englischen Münzen ist eine **Eiche** abgebildet.

   K A O R E E T ________ ________

5. Die **Harfe** gilt als ursprünglich irisches Musikinstrument. P R A H ____________

6. Der **Löwe** ist dreifach auf dem Fußballtrikot der englischen Nationalmannschaft abgedruckt. O N I L ____________

This sceptred isle

Invaders and conquerors

Über die Jahrhunderte war Großbritannien Ziel mehrerer Eroberungswellen. Wie gut kennen Sie sich damit aus?

1 

Celts

2 

Romans

3 

Vikings

4 

Normans

___ **A** Who replaced the English king with William the Conqueror in 1066?

___ **B** Who built Hadrian's Wall to keep out the 'wild people' of the North?

___ **C** A member of which group stepped on a thistle when they were trying to invade Scotland in the 13th century?

___ **D** Which people were pushed by the Anglo-Saxons into Wales, Scotland and Ireland, where their culture still lives on today?

___ **E** Which group had administrative control over a large part of North England (called 'the Danelaw') from the 9th century to the 13th century?

William Shakespeare hat Großbritannien in dem Drama *King Richard II* als **„this sceptred isle"** („diese hoheitliche Insel") beschrieben. Das Zepter (**sceptre**) stellt ein Herrschersymbol dar – damit wollte Shakespeare die politische Macht der Insel betonen, allerdings hauptsächlich die der englischen königlichen Dynastie.

Stories of the sea

Die englische Literatur ist bekannt für ihre Meeres- und Inselabenteuer. Ordnen Sie die Zusammenfassungen dem jeweils richtigen Buchtitel zu.

A Jim Hawkins finds a map. It shows where Captain Flint buried some treasure on an island. Jim and others go on a dangerous expedition to try to find it.

B One man is the only person alive after a shipwreck in the Caribbean. He is stranded on an island, where he manages to survive. He meets another man there and calls him 'Friday'.

C A ship's doctor discovers several island nations. In the most famous scene of the book, he is surrounded by tiny people who think he is a giant. He also meets mad scientists and talking horses.

D A group of schoolboys survive a plane crash on an island in the Pacific. They try to organise themselves, but the group gets out of control and the boys start being cruel and violent to each other.

Dressing for the weather

Das Inselklima bringt sehr wechselhaftes Wetter mit sich. Welche praktischen Accessoires sind hier versteckt?

1. Rubber boots named after a duke. TELLINGSNOW ____________

2. This will protect you from the rain. LABELRUM ____________

3. A long raincoat with a belt. CATCHTENOR ____________

4. You should wear these on your hands in cold weather. VELSOG ____________

This sceptred isle

Weather idioms

Es gibt im Englischen viele Redewendungen, die mit dem Wetter zu tun haben. Vervollständigen Sie die folgenden Beispiele mithilfe der Vorgaben.

1. It's a storm in a ______________________. *(Teetasse)*

   A tea glass **B** teapot **C** teabag **D** teacup

2. It's raining cats and ______________________. *(Hunde)*

   A hounds **B** dogs **C** foxes **D** mice

3. I'm feeling under the ______________________. *(Wetter)*

   A wetter **B** wether **C** weather **D** whether

4. This fog is a real ______________________-souper! *(Erbse)*

   A pea **B** bean **C** lentil **D** chicken

5. Every ______________________ has a silver lining. *(Wolke)*

   A rain **B** fog **C** cloud **D** shower

6. He had a face like ______________________ when he heard the news. *(Donner)*

   A storm **B** thunder **C** lightning **D** hail

„Großbritannien – da regnet es ja dauernd!“ Wer so schimpft, liegt falsch, denn die durchschnittliche Regenmenge ist auf der Insel kaum größer als in Deutschland. Anders ist allerdings die Schnelligkeit, mit der sich die Wetterlage ändern kann. Kein Wunder also, dass das Wetter ein sehr beliebtes Gesprächsthema ist.

Arriving in Britain

Gesucht werden englische Begriffe und Ortsnamen rund um die Einreise in Großbritannien.

WAAGRECHT →

3. Flughafen südlich von London
6. englisches Wort für „Flughafen"
11. einer der Londoner Hauptbahnhöfe
13. Bahnverbindung zum europäischen Festland
14. größter Flughafen Nordenglands
15. englisches Wort für „Zoll"
16. Paddington, Euston und St Pancras sind Londoner ... *stations*

SENKRECHT ↓

1. englisches Wort für „Reisebus"
2. englisches Wort für „Fähre"
4. Ankunftsbereich am Flughafen
5. Transferservice am Flughafen
7. unterirdische Verbindung zum Kontinent
8. Flughafen nördlich von London
9. einer der größten Flughäfen der Welt
10. englisches Wort für „Reisepass"
12. Hafenstadt mit weißen Klippen

London: a nation, not a city

London on a budget

So kann man in London für wenig Geld voll auf seine Kosten kommen:

- ☐ Der Eintritt zu den **großen Museen** ist generell kostenlos.
- ☐ Man kann für wenig Geld ein **Boris Bike** ausleihen.
- ☐ Riesige **Parks** (z. B. Hyde Park und St James' Park) bieten eine unbezahlbare Auszeit.
- ☐ Mit etwas Glück kann man kurz vor Vorstellungsbeginn günstige **Theatertickets** an der Theaterkasse bekommen.
- ☐ Während der Semesterferien bieten manche **Studentenwohnheime** günstige Übernachtungsmöglichkeiten.
- ☐ Preiswert einkaufen kann man auf **Flohmärkten** (wie z. B. Camden Market).

The Tube

Die **London Underground** – von Einheimischen **the Tube** genannt – ist die älteste U-Bahn der Welt und wurde 1863 eröffnet. Sie wird täglich von bis zu **3,4 Millionen Menschen** benutzt. Das schlichte Design des Liniennetzplans gehört zu den **Markenzeichen Londons** und wurde vielerorts nachgeahmt (z. B. in Berlin und Paris).

London: a nation, not a city

London facts

London ist eine Weltstadt der Superlative. Wie viel wissen Sie darüber schon?

1. More languages are spoken in London than in any other city in the world. How many?
   - ☐ **A** 25
   - ☐ **B** 100
   - ☐ **C** 250
   - ☐ **D** 750

2. Where can you look at the largest cut diamond (530 carats) in the world?
   - ☐ **A** Buckingham Palace
   - ☐ **B** Big Ben
   - ☐ **C** Tower of London
   - ☐ **D** British Museum

3. Where does Europe's biggest street carnival take place every year?
   - ☐ **A** Covent Garden
   - ☐ **B** Notting Hill
   - ☐ **C** Hyde Park
   - ☐ **D** Downing Street

4. The National Portrait Gallery has the largest portrait collection in the world. About how many pictures does the collection contain?
   - ☐ **A** 175
   - ☐ **B** 1,750
   - ☐ **C** 17,500
   - ☐ **D** 175,000

5. Which is Britain's largest department store, with over 90,000m^2 of selling space?
   - ☐ **A** Harrods
   - ☐ **B** Hamleys
   - ☐ **C** Fortnum & Mason
   - ☐ **D** Harvey Nichols

Travelling on the Tube

Was sollte man beachten, wenn man mit der Londoner U-Bahn unterwegs ist?

1. Most of the tourist attractions
2. Buy your ticket before you start your journey, because you can't
3. With a Travelcard or an Oyster Card you can
4. Each underground line
5. If you are travelling after midnight, you may need to

___ **A** has its own colour on the maps and signs.

___ **B** go by bus, because not all underground lines run all night.

___ **C** are in zones 1 and 2.

___ **D** buy tickets on the trains.

___ **E** save up to 50% of the normal ticket price.

Famous London sights

Kennen Sie diese Sehenswürdigkeiten? Verbinden Sie die Bilder mit dem jeweils richtigen Namen.

1

2

3

4

A Kew Gardens

B St Paul's Cathedral

C London Eye

D Houses of Parliament

Visiting London

Finden Sie die englischen Bezeichnungen für die beschriebenen Sehenswürdigkeiten.

1. Here you can visit a very famous Egyptian collection as well as the Rosetta Stone and the Elgin Marbles. RIBHITS ______ EMMUUS ______
2. This is Europe's busiest shopping street, in Mayfair. At Christmas time it has an impressive display of lights. FOXDOR ______ TEREST ______
3. It's not just the national stadium of England's soccer team, but also a venue for major rock concerts. BYELMWE ______ MADSUIT ______
4. This crosses the River Thames and can be opened to let ships pass through. WETOR ______ GRIBED ______

London: a nation, not a city

Who will you see where?

Wo in London würde man am ehesten diese Personen sehen?

A Mayfair

B Tower of London

C The Old Bailey

D Buckingham Palace

1

2

3

4

The East End

Im Osten Londons lag historisch gesehen das Armenviertel der Stadt, und auch heute unterscheidet sich dieser Stadtteil von anderen. Vervollständigen Sie den Text, um mehr über das East End herauszufinden.

Brick Lane used to be an area where bricks and **1.** ______________ were made. Over the **2.** ______________, different groups of **3.** ______________ came to live here – especially Huguenots, Jews and Bangladeshis – and today it is one of the most multicultural **4.** ______________ of London. Brick Lane is famous for its curry **5.** ______________ and other ethnic restaurants. At the Brick Lane Market on Sundays you can find really good **6.** ______________ for clothes if you look carefully. At the Old Truman Brewery, the 18th century industrial **7.** ______________ have been turned into creative spaces for art **8.** ______________ and various leisure and retail businesses.

A houses   B centuries   C tiles   D buildings

E galleries   F immigrants   G bargains   H parts

Welche Begriffe sind hier richtig? Alle vier Möglichkeiten reimen sich jeweils auf den gesuchten Cockney-Ausdruck, aber nur einer hat die richtige Bedeutung, die sich aus dem Kontext erschließen lässt.

Cockney rhyming slang

Der Londoner **Cockney**-Dialekt ist für seinen **Cockney rhyming slang** berühmt. Dabei wird das Wort, das man sagen möchte, durch einen Begriff ersetzt, der sich auf das betreffende Wort reimt. Statt **money** sagt man also **bread and honey**, was wiederum meist auf **bread** verkürzt wird. Teile dieser einstigen Geheimsprache werden heute überall in Großbritannien verstanden und verwendet.

1. How lovely to see you – I haven't seen you for **donkey's [ears]**!
   - ☐ A fears ☐ B piers
   - ☐ C beers ☐ D years

2. A man in the hotel was talking loudly to someone on his **dog and bone**.
   - ☐ A own ☐ B phone
   - ☐ C clone ☐ D stone

3. If the lift isn't working, you'll have to use the **apples [and pears]**.
   - ☐ A bears ☐ B fares
   - ☐ C stairs ☐ D shares

4. You need to use your **loaf [of bread]** to understand these complex instructions.
   - ☐ A head ☐ B bed
   - ☐ C dead ☐ D shed

Manche Stadtteile und Sehenswürdigkeiten haben irreführende Namen. Können Sie diese Beispiele vervollständigen?

Strange place names

1. You won't find clowns or acrobats here. — Piccadilly ____________
2. An attractive place but less green than its name. — Covent ____________
3. Something Egyptians use to sew with? — Cleopatra's ____________
4. This place is more expensive than the name suggests! — ____________side

A Needle B Cheap C Garden D Circus

Shop till you drop

Well-known chains

Manche Ketten gibt es fast in jeder Stadt.
Wo kann man welche Produkte kaufen?

1
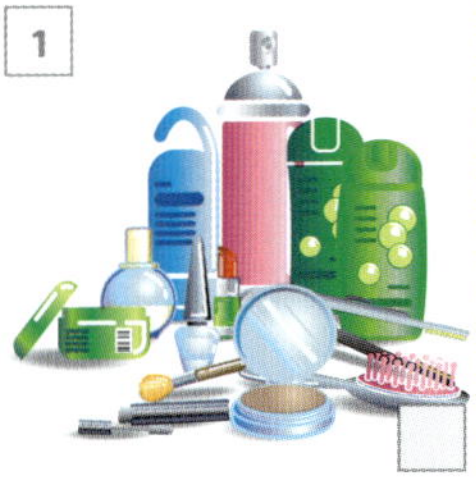

2

3

4

A WH Smith

B Mothercare

C Tesco

D Boots

Shop till you drop bedeutet etwa „Shoppen bis zum Umfallen“. Das geht besonders gut im größten städtischen Einkaufszentrum Europas, dem **Westfield Stratford City** im Osten Londons mit über 300 Geschäften, circa 70 Restaurants, einem Kino mit 14 Sälen, drei Hotels und dem größten Spielkasino Großbritanniens.

A nation of shopkeepers

Napoleon nannte die Briten einst verächtlich „eine Nation von Ladenbesitzern“. Aber wie heißen die Besitzer verschiedener Geschäften auf Englisch?

1. Someone who prepares and sells meat products. HERCTUB ____________
2. He or she will sell you fruit and vegetables. NERGEGECROR ____________
3. Who makes bread, cakes and pastries? KEBAR ____________
4. If you need a haircut, this person can help. DERIRHARESS ____________
5. Someone who sells flowers. ROFLSIT ____________

Opening hours

Was ist bei den britischen Ladenöffnungszeiten zu beachten?

1. On Sundays and public holidays,
2. In smaller towns and villages,
3. In most large supermarkets,
4. On Christmas Day and Easter Sunday,

___ **A** all shops are usually closed.

___ **B** many large shops are open.

___ **C** some shops close at 1 pm on one day of the week.

___ **D** you can do your shopping until 8 pm or 10 pm.

Charity shops

Gemeinnützige Gebrauchtwarenläden gibt es in fast allen Haupteinkaufsstraßen (**high streets**) britischer Städte. Was macht sie so beliebt?

1. Charity shops sell mainly ______________ clothes, books and household items.
2. These items are usually ______________ by people who live in the area.
3. The shops sell these things to raise money for people who are ______________, sick or underprivileged.
4. The prices are very ______________ – you can get some real bargains.
5. If you are lucky, you can sometimes find ______________ vintage clothing.
6. The people who run these shops are usually ______________ volunteers.

A reasonable **B** unpaid **C** second-hand

D donated **E** poor **F** high-quality

Eine der größten britischen **charities** ist **Oxfam,** die weltweit als Hilfs- und Entwicklungsorganisation tätig ist. Der erste **Oxfam shop** wurde 1947 in Oxford eröffnet; heute gibt es über 800 Läden in Großbritannien. Viele Promis unterstützen **Oxfam** (z. B. die Bands Coldplay und Die Toten Hosen).

Shop till you drop

Asking for help

Können Sie die Satzteile in die richtige Reihenfolge bringen?

1. Sie suchen eine Apotheke in der Nähe.
   you – me – tell – Could – is? – pharmacy – where – the nearest

   ____

2. Sie haben ein Kleidungsstück anprobiert, aber es ist zu groß.
   size. – a smaller – like to – I'd – I think – try

   ____

3. Sie möchten sich nach dem Rückgaberecht erkundigen.
   return – I – this – doesn't – if – Can – it – fit?

   ____

4. Sie fragen nach der Ladenschlusszeit.
   today? – you – do – what – close – time – At

   ____

In the department store

Können Sie herausfinden, was die hervorgehobenen Wörter bedeuten?

1. **Stationery:** writing paper, pens, pencils, diaries, calendars
2. **Lingerie:** women's underwear, nightdresses
3. **Haberdashery:** materials for sewing and handicrafts, fabrics
4. **Hosiery:** socks, stockings, tights

___ A Dessous ___ B Kurzwaren ___ C Strumpfwaren ___ D Schreibwaren

Buy British!

Bringen Sie die Buchstaben in die richtige Reihenfolge, um die Namen bekannter britischer Firmen herauszufinden.

1

WINGSTIN

____

2

RD TRAMNES

____

3

SLORL YEROC

____

4

FEDOVANO

____

Companies

Welche Aussage passt zu welcher der oben genannten Firmen?

___ **A** This manufacturer of strong footwear got the idea of putting air in the soles of shoes from a German army doctor.

___ **B** This company is closely connected with Britain's favourite hot drink. Its company logo has been in use since 1787.

___ **C** This is one of the largest telecommunications companies in the world. It has networks in over 30 countries.

___ **D** This company is best known for its luxury cars, but it also produces aeroplanes.

Westward Ho!

Cornish pasties

Wer schon mal in **Cornwall** war, wird kaum die vielen kleinen Läden übersehen haben, die diese **herzhaften Pasteten** verkaufen. Früher wurden sie von den Arbeitern in den **Zinnminen** verspeist, die unter Tage mit giftigen Substanzen zu tun hatten und die **pasties** am dicken Krustenrand festhalten konnten, ohne den leckeren Inhalt zu kontaminieren.

A strange name: Westward Ho!

Der Badeort **Westward Ho!** befindet sich an der Nordküste der Grafschaft Devon. Der Ort verdankt seinen merkwürdigen Ortsnamen einem gleichnamigen Roman, der im benachbarten Bideford spielt. Weltweit gibt es nur zwei Ortsnamen, die Ausrufezeichen beinhalten: die kanadische Stadt **Saint-Louis-du-Ha! Ha!** übertrumpft unseren mit gleich zwei davon!

Westward Ho!

Sights of the South West

Ordnen Sie die Beschreibungen den Fotos zu.

A This city in Somerset was built as a Roman spa town. It became very fashionable in the 18th century.

B Legends tell us that King Arthur lived at this castle on the coast of Cornwall.

C You will find this prehistoric structure in the county of Wiltshire. It was probably built for religious and astronomical reasons.

D This city in Devon has always been important for ships. Captain James Cook started several international expeditions from here.

Stonehenge

Tintagel

Plymouth

Bath

Which county is it?

Was gehört wohin?

1. The national ______________ Dartmoor and Exmoor can be found in Devon.
2. Somerset has a lot of agriculture and is famous for producing ______________ and cheese.
3. Cornwall once had its own language and is one of the Celtic ______________.
4. The coastline of Dorset contains cliffs and ______________ of great geological interest.
5. Stonehenge is one of many prehistoric ______________ in Wiltshire.

A nations

B rocks

C apples

D parks

E monuments

Welche Antwort stimmt?

Glastonbury fact file

1. The first Glastonbury Festival took place on 19th September 1970. This was the day after the death of which famous rock musician?
   ☐ A Elvis Presley ☐ B John Lennon ☐ C Jimi Hendrix ☐ D Freddy Mercury

2. According to legends, who brought the Holy Grail to Glastonbury?
   ☐ A Monty Python ☐ B King Arthur ☐ C archaeologists ☐ D Joseph of Arimathea

3. What exactly is Glastonbury Tor?
   ☐ A a kind of cake ☐ B a stupid person ☐ C a stone tower ☐ D a football club

4. Which local shoe manufacturer was the inspiration for The Shoe Museum in the town of Street near Glastonbury?
   ☐ A Hush Puppies ☐ B Birkenstock ☐ C Clarks ☐ D Manolo Blahnik

Welche der bereits erwähnten Grafschaften ist die einzige in England, die zwei voneinander getrennte Küstenlinien hat?

Coastlines

A Cornwall

B Devon

C Dorset

D Somerset

E Wiltshire

Answer: ____________________

Die uralte Siedlung **Glastonbury** in Somerset ist Legenden nach sowohl die wahre Stätte der mythischen Insel Avalon als auch Versteck des heiligen Grals. Sie ist deshalb schon seit Jahrhunderten beliebtes Ziel für Pilger und Touristen. Heutzutage zieht zudem das **Glastonbury Festival** jedes Jahr mehr als 100.000 Besucher an.

Westward Ho!

Cornish pasties

For the pastry:

450g flour
2 teaspoon baking powder
1 teaspoon salt
125g butter
2 egg yolks
125ml cold water

For the filling:

450g potatoes, finely dic
150g swede, finely diced
150g onions, finely choppe
300g beef rump steak,
finely chopped
1 tablespoon flour
40g butter
1 egg
salt and pepper

Lesen Sie das Rezept und vervollständigen Sie die Sätze.

1. For the pastry you need ______________, butter, egg yolks, baking powder, salt and ______________.
2. The ______________ is made out of meat and vegetables.
3. Most people make their pasties with finely chopped ______________ rump steak.
4. The vegetables most people use are ______________, swede and ______________.

Preparation method

Wie bereitet man **Cornish pasties** zu?
Bringen Sie die Sätze in die richtige Reihenfolge.

___ **A** Put some chopped vegetables and meat on each pastry circle.

___ **B** Bake the pasties in the oven for 50 minutes at 180°C.

___ **C** Mix the chopped steak with the flour, add salt and pepper and chop the vegetables. Then fetch your pastry from the fridge.

___ **D** Brush the edges of the circles with egg, then fold each circle over and seal the edges. Brush the tops of the pasties with egg and make a small hole in each one with a sharp knife.

___ **E** Roll out the chilled pastry and cut out six circles (each about 23 cm Ø).

___ **F** First, mix the pastry ingredients. Then put the pastry in the fridge for an hour while you prepare the other ingredients.

Food and drink

Welche typischen Lebensmittel sind hier versteckt?

1. An important element of cream tea. TELCODT MERAC ____________ ____________
2. A world-famous variety of cheese. HADDERC ________________
3. A popular alcoholic drink made out of Somerset apples. ICRED ________________
4. Many restaurants in Cornwall specialise in cooking this. DEOSOAF ________________

Fact or fiction?

Nur drei dieser skurrilen Aussagen sind nicht wahr. Finden Sie sie?

- ☐ **1.** Rosamunde Pilcher originally comes from Cornwall.
- ☐ **2.** More than 400 different kinds of apples are grown in Somerset.
- ☐ **3.** Cheddar cheese traditionally had to be made within 30 miles (48km) of Wells Cathedral.
- ☐ **4.** Surfing was invented in Newquay, Cornwall.
- ☐ **5.** A very famous and dangerous cheese-rolling competition takes place in Gloucestershire every year.
- ☐ **6.** The car journey from Land's End in Cornwall to John O'Groats in Scotland takes about 30 hours.
- ☐ **7.** The Tower of London would fit into the biggest greenhouse at the Eden Project.
- ☐ **8.** There are no lions in the South West of England.
- ☐ **9.** Most pirates in films speak with a South West English accent.
- ☐ **10.** The oldest rocks of the Jurassic Coast are 185 million years old.

Das **Eden Project** ist ein botanischer Garten in der Nähe von St Austell (Cornwall), der jährlich mehr als 1 Million Besucher anzieht. Er ist bekannt für seine bis zu 50 m hohen und 125 m breiten Gewächshäuser, in denen verschiedene Klima- und Vegetationszonen simuliert werden. Diese außerirdisch anmutenden Strukturen dienten als Kulisse für den James-Bond-Film *Die Another Day* (*Stirb an einem anderen Tag*).

Always look on the bright side

Humour

Der britische Humor ist weltberühmt. Von welchen bekannten Künstlern stammen diese Zitate?

1. "Better a witty fool than a foolish wit."
   (Tip: England's greatest dramatist)

2. "Satire is a sort of glass, wherein beholders do generally discover everybody's face but their own."
   (Tip: 18th-century Anglo-Irish satirist)

3. "You could read Kant by yourself, if you wanted; but you must share a joke with someone else."
   (Tip: Scottish author of *Treasure Island*)

4. "There is nothing in the world so irresistibly contagious as laughter and good humour."
   (Tip: English author of *A Christmas Carol*)

5. "Imagination was given to man to compensate him for what he is not; a sense of humour to console him for what he is."
   (Tip: English philosopher, statesman and author)

___ **A** Jonathan Swift ___ **B** Robert Louis Stevenson

___ **C** Charles Dickens ___ **D** Francis Bacon

___ **E** William Shakespeare

Wortwitz und Skurriles kommen in der britischen Literatur häufig vor. Besonders beliebte Beispiele sind etwa ***Alice's Adventures in Wonderland*** (1865) und ***Through the Looking-Glass, and What Alice Found There*** (1871) von **Lewis Carroll.** Das Unsinnsgedicht **„Jabberwocky"** aus letzterem Buch inspirierte 1977 den gleichnamigen Film von Monty Python-Mitglied Terry Gilliam. Sehr bekannt ist auch das Monty Python-Lied **„Always look on the bright side of life"** aus dem Film ***Life of Brian*** (1979).

Find the jokers

Suchen Sie anhand der Hinweise den passenden Namen oder Titel.

1. A comedy about working life which inspired the German series *Stromberg.*
2. Author of *The Hitchhiker's Guide to the Galaxy.*
3. John Cleese was a member of this famous comedy team.
4. This character wears a tweed jacket, pulls funny faces and is always making mistakes.
5. This comedian has played the characters Ali G, Borat and Brüno.
6. A comedy sketch series about eccentric British life.
7. This clay-animated character originally appeared in a film with Wallace and Gromit.
8. This sitcom was shown in Germany under the title *Mehr Schein als Sein.*

___ **A** Monty Python

___ **B** Sacha Baron Cohen

___ **C** *Little Britain*

___ **D** Shaun the Sheep

___ **E** *The Office*

___ **F** Douglas Adams

___ **G** *Keeping Up Appearances*

___ **H** Mr Bean

Comedy films

Zu welchen Filmen könnten diese Requisiten gehören?

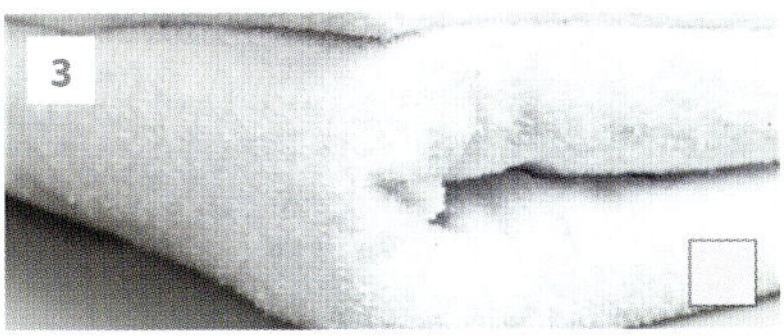

A *Monty Python and the Holy Grail*

B *Bridget Jones' Diary*

C *The Hitchhiker's Guide to the Galaxy*

D *Snatch*

Always look on the bright side

Jokes

Die einfachsten Witze bestehen nur aus einer Frage und einer Antwort. Welche Antwort passt hier zu welcher Frage?

Es gibt viele klassische Witzformate in Großbritannien, unter anderem **mother-in-law jokes** (meist böse Witze über Schwiegermütter) und **knock-knock jokes** (formelhafte Frage-Antwort-Wortspiele). Als **punchline** bezeichnet man die Pointe eines Witzes.

1. What is white when it's dirty and black when it's clean?
2. What travels around the world and stays in a corner?
3. What begins with 'p', ends with 'e' and has thousands of letters?
4. What do you call a boomerang that doesn't come back?
5. What has two legs but can't walk?
6. What can you hold without touching it?
7. What kind of apple isn't an apple?
8. What has a neck but no head?

___ A a stamp ___ B a blackboard ___ C a bottle ___ D a stick

___ E a pineapple ___ F half a dog ___ G post office ___ H a conversation

Describing humour

Bringen Sie die Buchstaben in die richtige Reihenfolge.

1. A joke that is RYDIT ______ is probably about sex.
2. Jokes that have a very dark side are called CLABK ______ humour.
3. Sarcastic or NORICI ______ comments are typical of British humour.
4. A remark that is TWITY ______ is clever and humorous at the same time.
5. The word 'funny' can mean either MINGAUS ______ or weird.
6. Something that is silly or foolish is URICIDSOUL ______.

Was passt hier nicht dazu?

Films and more

Die britische Firma **Aardman Animations** ist bekannt für ihre Knetanimationen. Sie gewann 1993 und 1995 Oscar-Auszeichnungen in der Kategorie „Bester animierter Spielfilm" für ihre Wallace und Gromit-Kurzfilme ***The Wrong Trousers*** und ***A Close Shave.*** Ihre Filme (z.B. ***Shaun the Sheep***) werden unter anderem auch in der *Sendung mit der Maus* ausgestrahlt.

1. Which of these animated productions is not a British creation?
   - ☐ A *Wallace and Gromit*
   - ☐ B *Bob the Builder*
   - ☐ C *The Simpsons*

2. Which actor was not a member of the Monty Python team?
   - ☐ A Terry Gilliam
   - ☐ B Rowan Atkinson
   - ☐ C John Cleese

3. Which of these comedy characters has not been played by a British actor?
   - ☐ A Austin Powers
   - ☐ B Johnny English
   - ☐ C Inspector Clouseau

4. Which of these TV productions is practically unknown in Britain?
   - ☐ A *Fawlty Towers*
   - ☐ B *Dinner for One*
   - ☐ C *The IT Crowd*

Restaurant jokes

Ein Witzformat besteht aus der Beschwerde oder Frage eines Restaurantgasts und der Antwort des Kellners. Welche Witzteile passen zusammen?

1. "Waiter, there is a fly in the butter!"
2. "Waiter, there's a dead fly swimming in my soup!"
3. "Waiter, do you have frogs' legs?"
4. "Waiter, there's a worm in my soup!"

___ A "No sir, I always walk like this."

___ B "Yes – sorry, sir, we didn't have any flies left."

___ C "Don't be silly, sir – dead flies can't swim!"

___ D "Yes sir, it's a butterfly."

It's grim up North – or is it?

The wild North of England

Wer einsame, raue Landschaft gerne mag, wird **Nordengland** lieben! Jenseits der Städte sind die **Nationalparks** beliebte Reiseziele. Hier sehen Sie den **Lake District,** aber vielleicht verschlägt es Sie ja auch in den **Peak District** oder in die **North York Moors**.

Better than its reputation

Der **Norden Englands** wird oft als industriell, kalt und grau beschrieben, also als **grim**. Der Einfluss der **industriellen Revolution** auf die Städte des Nordens ist zwar unverkennbar, aber heute findet man dort zudem ein durchaus **abwechslungsreiches Stadtleben** und **moderne Architektur** vor.

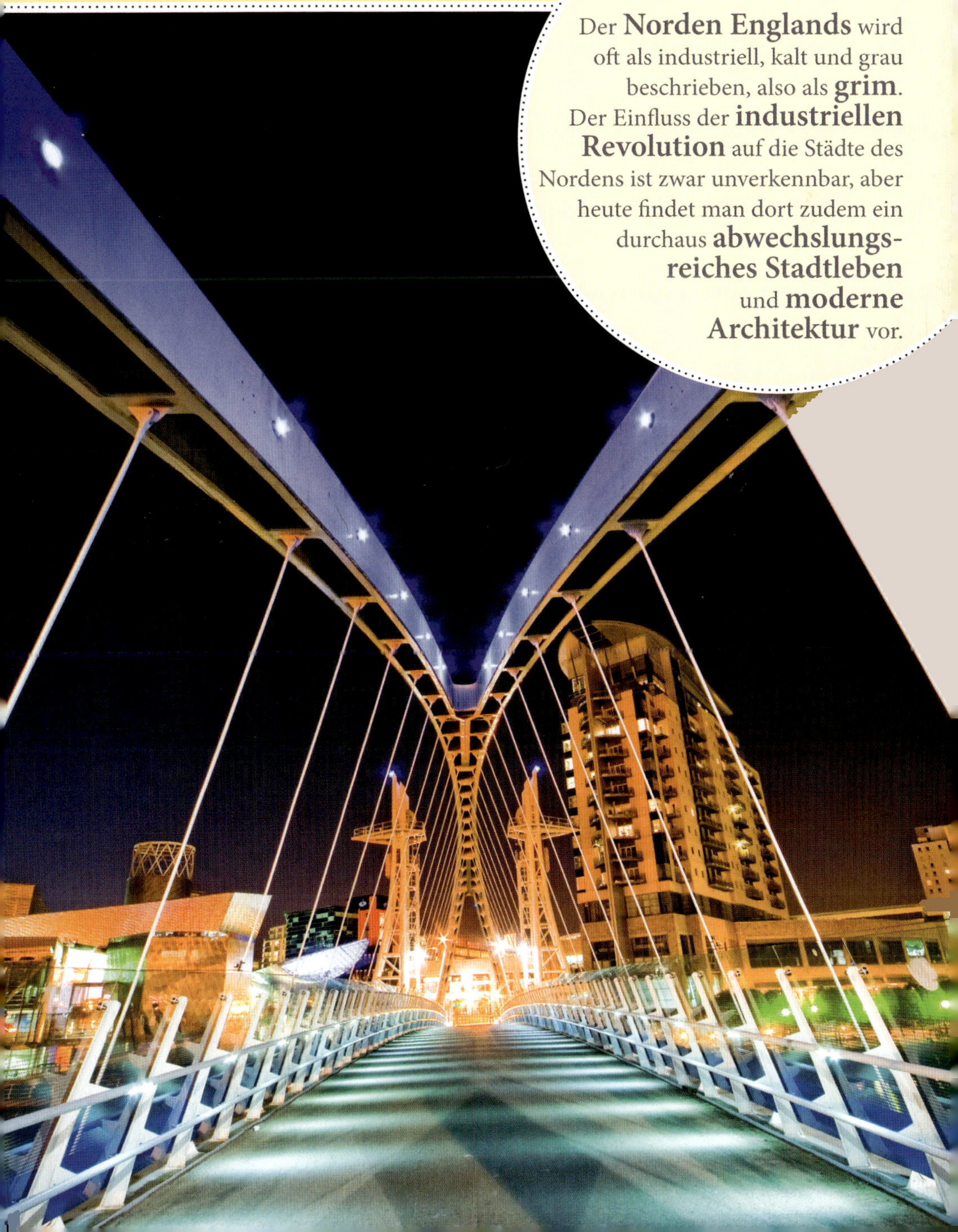

It's grim up North – or is it?

Cities of the North

ERMANCHESTERBIGLEEDSORESHEFFIELDSAINTOLIVERPOOLHAMNEWCASTLEVE

In der Wortschlange sind fünf Großstädte versteckt. Können Sie sie finden und auf der Landkarte richtig platzieren? Wählen Sie anschließend die passende Beschreibung für jede Stadt.

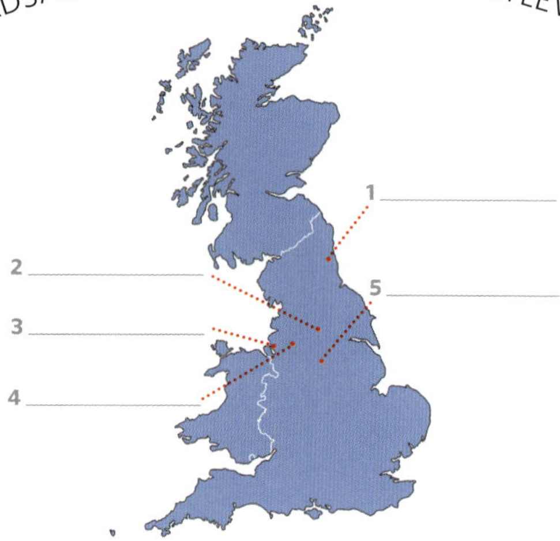

___ **A** One third of this steel-producing city in South Yorkshire lies within the Peak District national park. It also has the oldest football club in the world.

___ **B** This economic and cultural capital of the North East is located on the River Tyne at the eastern end of Hadrian's Wall.

___ **C** Home of the Beatles, this city near the Welsh border also has the fifth largest cathedral in the world.

___ **D** This city in West Yorkshire is the third largest in Great Britain – you will also find the largest fish and chips shop in the world near here!

___ **E** This location in North West England was the first industrial city in the world and home to the bands Simply Red, The Smiths and Oasis.

The industrial past

Was waren die traditionellen Industrien des Nordens?

1. Textile raw material that was imported from India and America. ___ **A** coal
2. An industry that is very suitable for an island. ___ **B** steelworks
3. The mining of this fossil fuel was affected by a big strike in 1984. ___ **C** cotton
4. Sheffield was once famous for its factories of this sort. ___ **D** shipbuilding
5. An important transport network in use before the railways. ___ **E** canals

Actors and singers

Kennen Sie diese Stars aus Nordengland? Ordnen Sie die Namen dem jeweils richtigen Bild zu.

A Judi Dench **B** Ian McKellen **C** Sting **D** Mel C

Tourist attractions

Erkennen Sie diese Sehenswürdigkeiten Nordenglands?

A Angel of the North

B Hadrian's Wall

C Blackpool Tower

D York Minster

Können Sie auch erraten, in welcher Reihenfolge diese gebaut wurden?

Reihenfolge: ______________________

It's grim up North – or is it?

Facts and figures

Nur eins der jeweils vorgeschlagenen Wörter hat die richtige Bedeutung.

1. **Blackpool Tower**
   It takes nine tons of **colour / paint** to cover the whole surface of Blackpool Tower. At the top of the tower, 154m **above / below** the ground, there is a transparent glass floor that you can walk on – if you are not afraid of heights!

2. **York Minster**
   York Minster is the biggest **medieval / middle-aged** cathedral north of the Alps. Its Great East Window is as **great / big** as a tennis court.

3. **Hadrian's Wall**
   Some people wrongly think that Hadrian's Wall marks the **limit / border** between England and Scotland. Today it is a popular destination for **wanderers / hikers**.

4. **Angel of the North**
   The wings of the Angel of the North measure 54m in total, making the sculpture **wider / taller** than a Boeing 757. It is Britain's largest sculpture and is believed to be the largest angel sculpture **in / of** the world.

The North-South divide

Vervollständigen Sie den Text.

The North of England is traditionally seen as more **1.** ____________ but financially less **2.** ____________ than the South, and in fact it is still true that there is more money and a **3.** ____________ standard of living in the South. The people of the North are described positively as **4.** ____________ and down-to-earth, and today the **5.** ____________ industry of the past has been replaced by lighter, more modern service industries. Many Northern cities now have a **6.** ____________ image with trendy nightlife as well as cultural and commercial attractions.

A higher | B friendly | C heavy | D industrial | E well-off | F fashionable

Food specialities

Einige Spezialitäten des Nordens sind nach deren Herkunftsort benannt. Können Sie die Ortsnamen der richtigen Speise zuordnen?

1. ____________ pudding: a side dish for roast beef made out of flour and eggs

2. ____________ sausage: a sausage in the shape of a snail

3. ____________ cake: a sweet pastry filled with currants

4. ____________ hotpot: a kind of lamb stew with potatoes

A Lancashire
B Cumberland
C Eccles
D Yorkshire

Northern brands

Einige bekannte Marken kommen aus dem Norden Englands. Können Sie diese Firmen mit dem jeweils richtigen Produkt verbinden?

1. John Smith	___	A sport clothing
2. Tetley	___	B beer
3. Reebok	___	C cars
4. Bentley	___	D tea

Im Norden Englands werden dunkle Biere wie **bitter** und **ale** bevorzugt. Bekannte Biermarken sind z. B. **John Smith** (das **extra smooth** dieser Brauerei ist landesweit die Nummer Eins unter den **ale**-Sorten) und **Newcastle Brown Ale.**

Meet the royals

Besonders bekann
ist das **Victorian age**
jenes Zeitalter also, da
sich mit der (bis dato!
längsten Regierungszei
eines britischen Monarche
deckt. Diese Epoche wa
geprägt von herausragende
Innovationen un
Fortschritt in Technik
Industrie und Gesellschaft
auch wenn die damalig
Moral aus heutiger Sich
eher steif und ver
klemmt erschein

Historical periods

Einige wichtige Epochen der englischen Geschichte sind mit der Regierungszeit eines oder mehrerer Monarchen verbunden. Können Sie die Bezeichnungen mit dem jeweils richtigen Zeitabschnitt verbinden?

1. 1485–1603 **2.** 1603–1714 **3.** 1811–1820

4. 1837–1901 **5.** 1901–1910

___ **A** Tudor ___ **B** Regency ___ **C** Edwardian

___ **D** Stuart ___ **E** Victorian

Politics and the monarchy

Für jede der oben genannten Epochen wird jetzt ein wichtiges politisches Ereignis genannt. Notieren Sie die Epoche, in der das betreffende Ereignis stattfand.

1. England became a republic for a short time, under Oliver Cromwell (1599–1658).
   ____
2. Henry VIII became the head of the Church of England after it separated from the Roman Catholic Church. ______________
3. Emmeline Pankhurst started a radical women's rights movement in the post-Victorian age.
   ____
4. This period began when the Prince of Wales, Georg Augustus Frederick of Hanover (1762–1830), took control of governing the country. ______________
5. During this period the Queen became the Empress of India and Britain was the most powerful country in the world. ______________

Official residences

Welches der Fotos zeigt **keine** offizielle Residenz der heutigen königlichen Familie?

1

Windsor Castle

2

Balmoral Castle

3

Buckingham Palace

4

Palace of Westminster

Royal sightseeing

Viele historische Residenzen und königliche Besitztümer können besichtigt werden, aber wo muss man hin, um was zu sehen?

1. Where were several members of the royal family imprisoned, including Elizabeth I?
   - ☐ A Hampton Court Palace
   - ☐ B Tower of London
   - ☐ C Buckingham Palace

2. Where can you have fun getting lost in the royal maze?
   - ☐ A Windsor Castle
   - ☐ B Hampton Court Palace
   - ☐ C Kensington Palace

3. Which residence has its own chapel, post office, doctor's surgery and cinema?
   - ☐ A Balmoral
   - ☐ B Key Palace
   - ☐ C Buckingham Palace

4. Which is the oldest castle in Europe that still has people living in it?
   - ☐ A Windsor Castle
   - ☐ B Palace of Westminster
   - ☐ C Tower of London

5. Which estate has a distillery that produces the Royal Lochnagar Single Malt whisky?
   - ☐ A Hampton Court Palace
   - ☐ B Balmoral
   - ☐ C Windsor Castle

Meet the royals

Royal ladies and gentlemen

Die Mitglieder der königlichen Familie tragen verschiedene Titel. Können Sie die Tabelle vervollständigen – links die männlichen Titel, rechts die weiblichen Entsprechungen?

1. GINK ________	queen
2. prince	SPECRINS ________
3. LERA ________	countess
4. duke	SCHUDES ________

The royal family

Wählen Sie das jeweils richtige Wort aus, um die Sätze zu ergänzen.

1. The Queen and her **man / husband**, Prince Philip, are both great-great grandchildren of Queen Victoria.
2. Before World War I, the royal family had no surname, but later they **adapted / adopted** the name Windsor.
3. Prince Charles has his own **brand / mark** of organic food products, called Duchy Originals.
4. The royal family follows the German tradition of opening their Christmas presents on Christmas **Day / Eve**, due to their German ancestry.
5. The royal family brings over 600 **million euros / millions of euro** into the UK every year through tourism.
6. Queen Elizabeth II has two **birthdays / dates of birth**: one in April and the official one in June.
7. The British monarch is not allowed to be married **to / with** someone who is Catholic.
8. More tourists travelled to the UK from Germany **as / than** any other country for the royal wedding of Prince William and Catherine Middleton on 29 April 2011.

Gesucht werden Namen, Titel und andere Begriffe rund um die königliche Familie.

More royal names and titles

ACROSS →

2. English word for "Krone".
3. Royal personality who was killed in 1997.
5. You should address the king or queen as "Your ..."
7. Most members of the royal family are addressed as "Your Royal ..."
9. Alliance of 53 states that has the British monarch as its head.
11. The father of Elizabeth II.

DOWN ↓

1. Eight kings have shared this first name.
2. Kate Middleton is now the Duchess of ...
4. The name of the Princess Royal, daughter of Elizabeth II.
6. The eldest son of Elizabeth II.
8. Father of princesses Eugenie and Beatrice.
10. Real first name of Prince Harry and of the king who had six wives in the 16th century.

Scotland the Brave

Scotland's national anthem(s)

Schottland hat drei inoffizielle Nationalhymnen und die bekannteste ist **„Scotland the Brave"**. Darin geht es hauptsächlich um die Schönheit der Landschaft und den Nationalstolz der Schotten:

Land of my high endeavour,
Land of the shining river,
Land of my heart for ever,
Scotland the brave.

Breathtaking landscapes

Neben den **höchsten Bergen Großbritanniens** (Ben Nevis: 1344 m) hat Schottland auch stolze **790 Inseln** und **1560 km² Lochs** (gälisches Wort für „Seen“).

Scotland the Brave

Scotland's economy

Welches Wort passt wohin?

1. Agriculture and __________ are the most important food-producing sectors for the Scottish economy.
2. The __________ distilleries in the Highlands and on the islands produce one of Scotland's best-known exports.
3. The energy industries include coal, North Sea gas and __________ .
4. In many parts of Scotland there are __________ industries such as banking, insurance and of course tourism.
5. Knitwear and __________ are traditional textile industries that are still important today.

A oil B tweed C whisky D fishing E service

Cities in Scotland

Können Sie die Städtenamen auf der Karte platzieren?

___ A Glasgow ___ B Inverness

___ C Edinburgh ___ D Dundee

___ E Aberdeen

Die Region zwischen Glasgow und Edinburgh ist heutzutage für ihre Hightechindustrie bekannt – man nennt sie deshalb auch **Silicon Glen**, in Anlehnung an das Silicon Valley in Kalifornien. **„Glen"** bedeutet „Tal" und kommt auch in vielen Ortsnamen oder nach diesen benannten Whiskymarken vor (z. B. **Glenfiddich** oder **Glenmorangie**).

Einiges ist anders in Schottland als im Rest Großbritanniens. Wie gut kennen Sie sich aus?

About Scotland

1. Scottish banks are allowed to produce their own ______________ . Be careful: some shops in England don't accept them!

   A coins *(Münzen)* B banknotes *(Geldscheine)* C currency *(Währung)*

2. Some Scottish men wear a ______________ on special occasions.

   A dress B skirt C kilt

3. Scotland has three official languages: English, Scots and Scottish ______________ .

   A garlic B Gallic C Gaelic

4. The New Year, more commonly known as ______________ in Scotland, is historically a more important celebration for Scots than Christmas.

   A Hogwarts B Hogmanay C mahogany

5. Scotland has the highest proportion of people with red ______________ in the world: 13% of the population, with 40% carrying the gene.

   A hair B eyes C hairs

Tourist destinations

Was ist hier zu sehen?

A Ardnamurchan Beach

B Glasgow Science Centre

C Glenmorangie Distillery

D Edinburgh Castle

Scotland the Brave

Inventive Scots

Wissen Sie, welcher Schotte was erfunden bzw. entdeckt hat?

1. surgical use of antiseptics (1865)
2. telephone (patented 1876)
3. pneumatic tyres (patented 1888)
4. television (1922)
5. penicillin (1928)

___ A John Logie Baird (1888–1946)

___ B Alexander Fleming (1881–1955)

___ C Joseph Lister (1827–1912)

___ D Alexander Graham Bell (1847–1922)

___ E John Boyd Dunlop (1840–1921)

Scottish culture

Können Sie die versteckten Wörter enträtseln?

1. A Scottish hero, William ..., as seen in the film *Braveheart*. — LACLAWE ______
2. A kind of biscuit made out of flour, butter and sugar. — BARDSOTHER ______
3. A Scottish dish, made of sheep's stomach filled with meat, oats and herbs. — GIGSAH ______
4. The part of Scotland where the highest mountains are. — GHALDSHIN ______
5. A very loud musical instrument. — GABPEPSI ______
6. Nickname for the Loch Ness Monster. — SENISE ______

Haggis gilt zwar als typisch schottisch, aber es gibt schon seit der Antike ähnliche Gerichte in anderen Ländern. **Haggis** wird besonders gern am 25. Januar zur **Burns Night** gegessen, dem Geburtstag des schottischen Nationalpoeten **Robert Burns** (1759–1796). In seinem Gedicht „Address to a Haggis" preist er dessen Einzigartigkeit: „Fair fa' your honest, sonsie face, Great chieftain o' the puddin-race!"

Scottish words

Können Sie die Bedeutung der fett gedruckten Wörter aus dem Kontext richtig erraten?

1. I can't drink more than a **wee** glass of whisky as I have to do some work later.
   ☐ A strong ☐ B small
   ☐ C large ☐ D full

2. Fiona's a busy mum because she has three small **bairns** to look after.
   ☐ A shops ☐ B dogs
   ☐ C children ☐ D husbands

3. That's a very **bonny** photo of you – you look so relaxed and happy.
   ☐ A attractive ☐ B bad
   ☐ C small ☐ D funny

4. Would you like some boiled **tatties** with your haggis?
   ☐ A salad ☐ B tea
   ☐ C sheep ☐ D potatoes

5. "Is this the bus to Glasgow?" – "**Aye**, that's right!"
   ☐ A No ☐ B Yes ☐ C Maybe ☐ D Hello

Scotland fact file

Verbinden Sie die Satzhälften richtig, um fünf Fakten über Schottland herauszufinden.

1. There is no proof that ___
2. It has become a tradition that ___
3. Since 1 July 1999 ___
4. Even though it is Scotland's capital, ___
5. Although Scotland was never part of the Roman Empire, ___

A a Scotsman wears nothing under his kilt.

B Edinburgh is smaller than Glasgow.

C Scottish law is based on Roman law.

D the Loch Ness Monster exists.

E Scotland has had its own parliament.

In Schottland wird die Schreibweise **whisky** verwendet, im Gegensatz zu der in Irland und den USA gängigen Form **whiskey.** Das Wort stammt vom gälischen **„uisge beatha“** („Wasser des Lebens“). Außerdem unterscheidet man zwischen **blended whisky** aus gemischten Destillaten und dem begehrten, ungemischten **single malt.**

This sporting life

British sport

Ordnen Sie die Aussagen dem jeweils richtigen Namen zu.

1. An elite school that gave its name to a sport.
2. A famous location for horse racing in Berkshire.
3. National stadium of the England football team.
4. This elite school owns a rowing lake that was used during the 2012 London Olympics.
5. The oldest and best-known tennis tournament in the world takes place here.
6. This city has football clubs with 'United' and 'City' in their names.
7. The surname of the first British winner of the Tour de France.
8. The 'home of golf' with the oldest golf course in the world.

___ A Wembley

___ B St Andrews

___ C Eton

___ D Wimbledon

___ E Manchester

___ F Wiggins

___ G Rugby

___ H Ascot

History of sport

Ordnen Sie jedes Bild der richtigen Beschreibung zu.

tennis

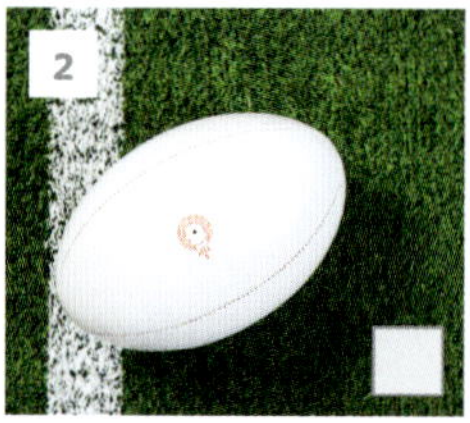

rugby

cricket

football

A This is an ancient game. Today it is played by over 250 million players in over 200 countries, making it the world's most popular sport.

B This sport originated in France. In the 16th century, people started using racquets instead of their hands to hit the ball.

C The rules for this game were developed in the 19th century. It is quite similar to American Football. It is also popular in France, Italy, New Zealand and South Africa.

D This game using a bat and ball goes back to medieval times. Today it is popular in many Commonwealth countries such as Australia, the West Indies and Pakistan.

Der Originaltitel des in deutschsprachigen Ländern als ***Kick It Like Beckham*** bekannten Fußballfilms war ***Bend It Like Beckham***. „Bend" bedeutet „krümmen" und ist hier eine Anspielung auf die Art und Weise wie David Beckham seine Flanken spielt.

Sport in films

Alle fünf Filme wurden in Großbritannien gedreht. Um welche Sportart geht es jeweils?

1. *Fever Pitch* (1997)
2. *Chariots of Fire (Die Stunde des Siegers,* 1981)
3. *Match Point* (2005)
4. *Billy Elliot* (2000)
5. *Flying Scotsman (Allein zum Ziel,* 2006)

___ A tennis

___ B dancing

___ C cycling

___ D football

___ E running

Rules of the game

Wie gut kennen Sie sich mit den Spielregeln dieser Sportarten aus?

1. In which game is zero points called **'love'**, while a score of 40-40 is called **'deuce'**? ___
2. In which sport are the points called **'runs'**, with a hundred runs being a **'century'**? ___
3. In which two of these games do the players traditionally wear **white clothing**? ___
4. In which game are you allowed to throw the ball **backwards** only? ___
5. Which sport has the **FA Cup** competition every year? ___
6. In which game do you get three points when you score a **try**? ___
7. In which sport is there always one **bowler** and two **batsmen**? ___
8. In which game do you often hear the term **'offside'**? ___

A tennis B rugby C football D cricket

This sporting life

Idioms from sport

Verbinden Sie jede Redewendung mit der richtigen Übersetzung.

1. The bad news really knocked our team for six.
2. I think I scored an own goal at the meeting today.
3. We managed to close a hat-trick of deals this week.
4. There was a real sense of fair play in the group.
5. Our boss showed him the red card for breaking his contract.
6. We'll have to wait now: the ball is in our partner company's court.

___ A Diese Woche haben wir es geschafft, drei Verträge abzuschließen.

___ B Jetzt müssen wir erstmal abwarten, unsere Partnerfirma ist am Zug.

___ C In der Gruppe gab es einen ausgeprägten Sinn für Fairness.

___ D Die schlechte Nachricht erschütterte unsere Abteilung zutiefst.

___ E Ich glaube, ich habe mir heute während der Besprechung ein Eigentor geschossen.

___ F Unsere Chefin hat ihm wegen Vertragsbruch gekündigt.

Sport vocabulary

Bringen Sie die Buchstaben in die richtige Reihenfolge.

1. A group of teams who play against each other. ALEGUE ____________
2. The building where football matches take place. DATUMIS ____________
3. Someone who trains sportsmen and -women. HACCO ____________
4. The final score at the end of a game. ERSTUL ____________
5. The grass area where many team ball games are played. THIPC ____________
6. Shoes people often wear for sport. RARESNIT ____________
7. The name for the area where you play tennis, badminton or squash. UCTOR ____________
8. You wear these so that you can see underwater. GELGOGS ____________

Das Wort **penalty** hat zwei verschiedene Bedeutungen im Sport. In vielen Sportarten bezeichnet es eine Strafe in Form von Punkt- oder Zeitabzug. Beim Fußball dagegen bedeutet es einen Elfmeter (was aber für die gegnerische Mannschaft wiederum ein Strafstoß ist).

Disciplines

Versteckt sind acht Sportarten, die aus Großbritannien stammen. Die Bilder helfen Ihnen dabei.

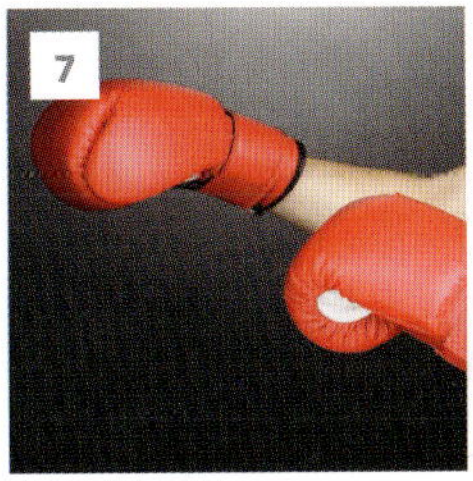

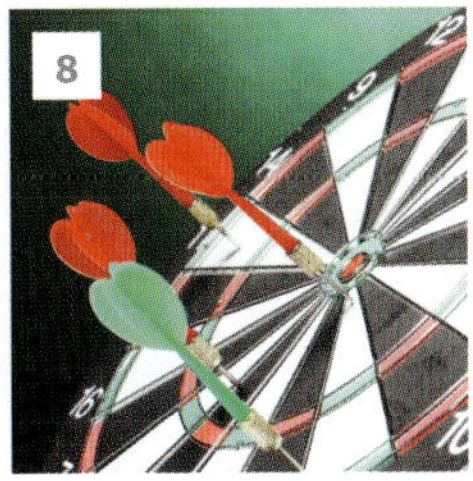

D	T	E	U	Q	O	R	C	F	E
O	J	R	R	W	E	A	A	Y	U
D	Y	B	A	S	E	B	A	L	L
H	S	A	U	Q	S	I	J	P	U
W	B	A	D	M	I	N	T	O	N
G	R	W	X	Y	M	A	S	O	X
O	O	P	B	V	H	O	T	L	Q
L	P	F	L	I	X	F	R	P	B
F	J	W	T	P	T	E	A	E	T
B	O	X	I	N	G	P	D	L	I

Wales – the Land of Song

"Of poets and singers"

Die walisische Nationalhymne preist **die musischen Elemente** der Kultur, und schon seit dem Mittelalter sind die Waliser für ihren Gesang berühmt. Auch heute gibt es vielerorts **Chöre**, und **Bands** wie Catatonia, Super Furry Animals oder die Stereophonics sind international bekannt.

A loooong placename

Einer der **längsten Ortsnamen der Welt** gehört einem kleinen Dorf auf der walisischen Insel Anglesey. Übersetzt heißt er: „Marienkirche in einer Mulde weißer Haseln in der Nähe eines schnellen Wirbels und der Tysiliokirche bei der roten Höhle“.

The Land of Song

Wales

Fünf dieser Aussagen sind wahr, die anderen basieren auf weit verbreiteten Missverständnissen.

		TRUE	FALSE
1.	Wales has three times as many sheep as human residents.	☐	☐
2.	Some people here speak Gaelic, like the Scots.	☐	☐
3.	Wales has 1200km of public paths around its coastline.	☐	☐
4.	Wales is seen today as a part of England.	☐	☐
5.	Mount Everest was named after a Welshman.	☐	☐
6.	Wales has the highest concentration of castles anywhere in Europe.	☐	☐
7.	There are parts of Wales where local people do not speak English.	☐	☐
8.	Wales does not have its own national football team.	☐	☐
9.	You have to pay to enter Wales using the bridge over the River Severn.	☐	☐
10.	Since Wales is a very rural region, there has been hardly any industry there.	☐	☐

Welsh slate

Die Geschichte der Schieferindustrie in Wales bietet einige Überraschungen. Vervollständigen Sie den Text.

The history of the slate industry in Wales goes back to the Roman **1.** ____________. During the Industrial **2.** ____________, it became very important in the 19th **3.** ____________. The two biggest slate **4.** ____________ in the world were at Penrhyn and Dinorwic, and they manufactured tiles for **5.** ____________ as well as material for floors and gravestones. In 1898, about 17,000 **6.** ____________ were employed in the industry, which produced 500,000 **7.** ____________ of slate that year. When part of Hamburg was destroyed by a big **8.** ____________ in 1842, Welsh slate was bought to re-roof its buildings.

- **A** century
- **B** tons
- **C** Revolution
- **D** roofs
- **E** Empire
- **F** quarries
- **G** workers
- **H** fire

Welsh celebrities

Wer ist für was bekannt? Ordnen Sie die Namen dem richtigen Beruf zu.

1. Catherine Zeta Jones	___	A fashion designer
2. Tom Jones	___	B film director
3. Laura Ashley	___	C actress
4. Peter Greenaway	___	D opera singer
5. Bryn Terfel	___	E pop singer

Jones ist der häufigste Familienname in Wales. Wie viele walisische Nachnamen (z. B. **Evans, Davies, Williams**) basiert er auf der Genitivform eines männlichen Vornamens (hier: **John**). Ähnlich wie in Skandinavien wurden die Leute früher als „Sohn / Tochter von XY" identifiziert; erst später wurden diese Formen zu tradierten Familiennamen.

Sightseeing in Wales

Die Bilder zeigen einige Sehenswürdigkeiten in Wales. Können Sie sie dem jeweils richtigen Namen zuordnen?

1

2

3

4

A Caernarvon Castle

B St David's Cathedral

C Mount Snowdon

D Talyllyn Railway

The Land of Song

Facts about Wales

In jeder dieser Aussagen über Wales ist nur eins der vorgeschlagenen Wörter richtig.

1. Laverbread is a Welsh **specialisation / speciality** made of seaweed.
2. The National **Library / Bibliography** in Aberystwyth owns more than four million books.
3. Around 20% of the population of Wales can **speak / talk** Welsh.
4. You can **drive / travel** by train to the top of Mount Snowdon.
5. Many Welsh **seaside / bath** resorts have beautiful sandy beaches.
6. You can go by ferry to Ireland from **havens / ports** such as Holyhead and Fishguard.
7. Welsh is one of the **oldest / eldest** living languages in Europe.
8. Many **foreign / outlandish** companies have factories in South Wales and offices in the capital, Cardiff.

A Welsh snack

Lesen Sie das Rezept für **Welsh rarebit** und beantworten Sie die Fragen dazu.

Ingredients

225g Cheddar cheese, grated
25g butter
1 teaspoon mustard
60ml brown ale
salt and pepper
4 slices of bread

Preparation

Put the cheese, butter, mustard and beer in a saucepan over a low heat. Stir until the cheese is melted and the mixture is smooth. Add salt and pepper.
Toast the bread and then spread the cheese mixture onto each of the slices. Put it under a pre-heated grill until it is golden brown in colour.

1. Der Käse sollte
   - ☐ **A** in Scheiben sein.
   - ☐ **B** gerieben sein.

2. Was für ein Bier wird benötigt?
   - ☐ **A** helles
   - ☐ **B** dunkles

3. Worin werden die Zutaten erhitzt?
   - ☐ **A** in einem Topf
   - ☐ **B** in der Pfanne

4. Welche Konsistenz soll die Käsemischung haben?
   - ☐ **A** glatt
   - ☐ **B** klumpig

5. Wo wird das Gericht fertig gestellt?
   - ☐ **A** auf dem Grill
   - ☐ **B** unter dem Grill

Welsh and German

Es gibt Wörter in der walisischen Sprache, die ihren deutschen Entsprechungen stark ähneln. Können Sie die Bilder mit dem jeweils richtigen Wort verbinden? Finden Sie anschließend die englischen Übersetzungen in der unten stehenden Wortschlange.

1  ☐

2  ☐

3  ☐

4  ☐

A cloch **B** moron **C** ffenestr **D** cwningen

GAREWINDOWNUMBELLITTERABBITHERMALCARROTSELF

Highest, longest, largest

Hier sind einige Namen zu enträtseln, die in diesem Kapitel bereits erwähnt wurden.

1. The longest river in Britain starts in Wales.
   NEVERS ________________
2. The largest city and the capital of Wales.
   FRADCIF ________________
3. The highest mountain in Wales.
   WONDSON ________________
4. The smallest city in Britain.
   TS VIDD'AS ___ ________________

Das kleinste Haus Großbritanniens ist das rote **Quay House** in Conwy an der nordwalisischen Küste. Es ist 3,05 m hoch und 1,90 m breit. Der letzte Bewohner (bis 1900) war ein 1,90 m großer Fischer namens Robert Jones.

On the roads and rails

Road signs

Können Sie die Bedeutung dieser Straßenschilder erraten?

1

- ☐ **A** Sie müssen den Weg räumen.
- ☐ **B** Sie haben Vorfahrt.
- ☐ **C** Sie haben keine Vorfahrt.
- ☐ **D** Achtung Gehweg.

2

- ☐ **A** Vorne kommt eine Kirche.
- ☐ **B** Die Fahrbahn wird schmäler.
- ☐ **C** Achtung Altglascontainer.
- ☐ **D** Weiter vorne kommt ein Tunnel.

3

- ☐ **A** Jetzt schneller fahren.
- ☐ **B** Ende des Tempolimits.
- ☐ **C** Jetzt langsamer fahren.
- ☐ **D** Verkehrsberuhigte Zone.

4

- ☐ **A** Hier darf man jederzeit parken.
- ☐ **B** Ausfahrt Tag und Nacht freihalten.
- ☐ **C** Durchfahrt jederzeit möglich.
- ☐ **D** Durchgehendes Parkverbot.

Wenn Sie vorhaben in Großbritannien Auto zu fahren, sollten Sie davor die britische Straßenverkehrsordnung (**Highway Code**) lesen, die alle Verkehrsregeln und -schilder erläutert. Sie ist im Buchhandel und in Fremdenverkehrsbüros (**Tourist Information Centres**) erhältlich.

5

- ☐ **A** Vorne kommt ein Recyclinghof.
- ☐ **B** Rechter Hand befindet sich eine Wendeplatte.
- ☐ **C** Vorne kommt ein Kreisverkehr.
- ☐ **D** Achtung geänderter Verkehrsfluss.

Vocabulary of driving

Ordnen Sie die Begriffe rund um den Straßenverkehr den deutschen Übersetzungen zu.

1. motorway
2. safety belt
3. speed limit
4. roundabout
5. dual carriageway
6. petrol
7. parking meter
8. roadworks
9. diversion
10. traffic lights
11. lane
12. driving licence

___ A Straßenarbeiten
___ B Fahrspur
___ C Umleitung
___ D Kreisverkehr
___ E zweispurige Fahrbahn
___ F Autobahn
___ G Tempolimit
___ H Sicherheitsgurt
___ I Sprit
___ J Führerschein
___ K Ampel
___ L Parkuhr

Linksverkehr herrscht überall in Großbritannien und Irland. Es gibt verschiedene Erklärungen dafür, aber eine der gängigsten ist, dass man früher etwaigen Feinden mit der Waffe in der rechten Hand begegnen wollte.

Rules of the road

Können Sie die Satzhälften richtig miteinander verbinden und so einige wichtige Verkehrsregeln entdecken?

1. A double yellow line at the side of the road means that
2. It is absolutely essential that
3. On motorways, remember that
4. Cyclists need to be careful because
5. As a pedestrian, don't forget that

___ A the speed limit is 70mph (112kmh).
___ B not all towns and cities have bike lanes.
___ C you cannot park there at any time.
___ D all car passengers wear safety belts.
___ E you look to the right first before you cross the road.

On the roads and rails

Using public transport

Was ist die richtige Lösung?

1. I'd like a ______________ *(hin und zurück)* ticket to Leeds, please.
   A single B day C season D return
2. Which ______________ *(Gleis)* do I need for the train to Edinburgh?
   A hall B station C platform D service
3. Is it possible to reserve a ______________ *(Sitzplatz)*?
   A seat B place C chair D space
4. The ticket machine is ______________ *(außer Betrieb)*, so can I buy a ticket on the train?
   A out of time B out of order C out of luck D out of the office
5. I'm pleased that the bus was ______________ *(pünktlich)* this morning.
   A out of time B on time C late D delayed
6. Unfortunately my train had a ______________ *(Verspätung)* of half an hour.
   A delay B connection C breakdown D journey time

Saving money

Entschlüsseln Sie die fehlenden Wörter, um nützliche Tipps zu erhalten.

1. It is HAPREEC ______________ to travel between 09:30–17:00 and after 19:00.
2. Buying train tickets in VENDACA ______________ can also save you money.
3. If you are travelling with several people, ask if there is a group CONSIDUT ______________.
4. A return ticket often costs a lot less than two GLINES ______________ tickets.
5. RHILDCEN ______________ under the age of five often travel free on public transport and there are usually reductions for anyone under 16.

More public transport

Weitere Transportmittel stehen hier im Stau. Hinweise dazu befinden sich unten.

INCOACHEERCABLEDECKERUNCONDUCTORFITTEREXPRESSOCONNECTIONABLE

1. Dieses Wort bedeutet sowohl „Reisebus" als auch „Waggon": ______________.
2. Ein doppelstöckiger Bus heißt auf Englisch „double-______________".
3. Eine anderes Wort für Taxi ist ______________.
4. So heißt eine Reiseverbindung (z. B. bei einer Zugfahrt) auf Englisch: ______________
5. Er oder sie kontrolliert die Fahrscheine im Zug oder in der Straßenbahn: ______________
6. National ______________ ist das größte landesweite Reisebusunternehmen.

Taxi!

Was sollte man beim Taxifahren beachten?

1. You can ask the hotel reception to ______________ a taxi for you.
2. All airports and main railway stations have a taxi ______________ outside.
3. The ______________ shows you how much you need to pay.
4. If the "For ______________" sign is lit up, the taxi is available.
5. The ______________ is the total cost of your journey.

A rank **B** meter **C** fare **D** call **E** hire

Wer in London Taxifahrer(in) werden will, muss eine extrem harte Prüfung bestehen. Sie heißt **The Knowledge** (Das Wissen) und sorgt dafür, dass die **cabbies** ohne Karten, Navi oder Funkkontakt ihre Passagiere möglichst schnell ans Ziel bringen. Die meisten brauchen mindestens 34 Monate und 12 Versuche, um den Test zu bestehen.

Do you fancy a drink?

Signs of the times

Die **traditionellen Kneipenschilder** in Großbritannien gehen auf einen Erlass aus dem Jahr 1393 zurück. Damals konnten die meisten Leute nicht lesen und Bilder waren daher gute Identifizierungsmerkmale für die **Pubs**.

Tea: the British elixir of life

Laut dem **United Kingdom Tea Council** werden täglich **165 Millionen Tassen Tee** in Großbritannien getrunken. Pro Kopf ergibt das 1,89 kg losen Tee pro Jahr. Noch größer ist der Teekonsum in Irland, mit 3,22 kg pro Kopf im Jahr.

Do you fancy a drink?

Der Ritus des heiligen Fünfuhrtees entspricht heute nicht (mehr) den Gewohnheiten des Alltags, aber man kann sich trotzdem ab und zu mit einem **afternoon tea** oder **cream tea** verwöhnen (z. B. während eines Kurzurlaubs). Aber nicht wundern, wenn Sie davon gut satt werden, denn es kann üppig werden!

Tea break

Welches Wort gehört wohin?

Most cups of tea in Britain are made with **1.** ____________, and PG Tips is the most popular brand. Generally people drink black tea, usually with **2.** ____________ and sometimes with sugar. At home and at work, tea is generally served in a **3.** ____________ rather than a delicate cup and **4.** ____________, and **5.** ____________ are an essential feature of the working day: **6.** ____________ are entitled to a 20-minute break for every six **7.** ____________ they work. More people have a **8.** ____________ at work than a coffee machine.

A mug	B hours	C employees	D milk
E tea bags	F saucer	G kettle	H tea breaks

Afternoon tea

Was wird zum **afternoon tea** eher nicht serviert?

1

Victoria sponge

2

sandwiches

3

filled baguette

4

scones

The tea ceremony

Lesen Sie die Anweisung zur Teezubereitung und entscheiden Sie, ob die unten stehenden Aussagen richtig oder falsch sind.

First, pour boiling water into the tea pot to warm it, and then pour it away. Add teaspoons full of loose tea to the pot: the quantity should be one teaspoon per person and one extra for the pot. Next, add freshly boiled water to the pot and let the tea brew for a few minutes. You can pour milk into the cup either before or after the tea is poured. Allow your guests to add their own sugar, if they would like it.

	TRUE	FALSE
1. Die Teekanne sollte zuerst mit kochendem Wasser angewärmt werden.	☐	☐
2. Die losen Teeblätter sollten mit einem Esslöffel pro Person dosiert werden.	☐	☐
3. Man lässt das Wasser etwas abkühlen, bevor es in die Kanne kommt.	☐	☐
4. Die Milch wird wahlweise vor oder nach dem Tee in die Tasse gegossen.	☐	☐
5. Man sollte nicht vergessen, jedem Gast etwas Zucker in den Tee zu geben.	☐	☐

Tea quiz

Testen Sie Ihr Wissen rund um das Thema „Tee“.

1. LARE YERG ______________ is a tea named after a British prime minister.
2. The main type of tea used in most British tea bags is SAMAS ______________.
3. Some people prefer fruit tea or BREAHL __________ tea to black or green tea.
4. The SETA DIANI ________________ Company was a famous importer of tea.
5. English KREBSFAAT _______________ tea is a popular blend of tea.
6. NOCSSE _______________ are small bread-like cakes, sometimes with raisins, often served with afternoon tea.

Do you fancy a drink?

Pub culture

Wie gut kennen Sie die britische Kneipenkultur?

1. In British pubs, you usually order food and drinks

   ☐ A from the waiter / waitress. ☐ B at your table. ☐ C at the bar. ☐ D online.

2. If you want to order a large beer (about 0.5l), you say "A ... of beer, please".

   ☐ A glass ☐ B large ☐ C half ☐ D pint

3. You have to pay for your drinks

   ☐ A when you arrive. ☐ B when you order them.
   ☐ C when they are brought to your table. ☐ D just before you leave.

4. If you are at the pub with people you know, it is normal to buy drinks

   ☐ A separately. ☐ B in rounds. ☐ C for strangers. ☐ D with a credit card.

5. If you want to smoke a cigarette, you can do this

   ☐ A at the bar. ☐ B anywhere.
   ☐ C in the smoking room. ☐ D outside in the smoking area.

Pub snacks

Welches Bild passt zu welchem Begriff? Und was davon würde man in einem Pub eher nicht bekommen?

1  ☐

2  ☐

3  ☐

4  ☐

A pork scratchings

B peanuts

C crisps

D pretzel

Usually not served in pubs: ____________________

Beer types

Verschiedene Biersorten sehen unterschiedlich aus. Welches Wort passt zu welchem Bild?

1

2

3

A lager (e.g. Carling) B bitter (e.g. John Smith's) C stout (e.g. Guinness)

Drinks with little or no alcohol

Welche Beschreibung passt zu welchem Getränk?

1. This sounds like a kind of beer, but it is non-alcoholic.
2. This is a mixture of beer and lemonade.
3. You need to add water to this concentrated fruit syrup.
4. A sweet drink that contains no sugar.
5. This is a mixture of wine and sparkling water.

__ A shandy

__ B squash / cordial

__ C diet cola / diet lemonade

__ D spritzer

__ E ginger ale

Small talk at the pub

Im Pub kommt man leicht miteinander ins Gespräch. Können Sie diese Redewendungen vervollständigen?

1. Can I ________ you a drink?
2. You're on your own – would you like to ________ us?
3. Which beer would you ________?
4. It's very full in here – do you ________ if we share your table?
5. Do you ________ here regularly?
6. Let's ________ what this beer tastes like – cheers!

A recommend

B come

C mind

D buy

E join

F see

Glorious grub

British food brands

Welche britische Marken gibt es für diese Lebensmittelprodukte?

1  ☐

2  ☐

3  ☐

4  ☐

A Weetabix

B Patak's

C McVitie's

D Cadbury

Als typisch britisches Produkt gilt **Marmite** – ein sehr salziges Hefeextrakt, das meistens als Brotaufstrich verwendet wird. Bekanntester und sehr treffender Werbespruch dieses Produkts ist „Love it or hate it". Laut Statistik nehmen etwa 25% der Briten **Marmite** mit, wenn sie einen längeren Auslandsaufenthalt planen.

Eating internationally

Welche Nationalitäten beeinflussen durch ihre Küche den britischen Speiseplan heutzutage am stärksten? Die Top 5 sind hier versteckt.

MARCHINESEREVINDIANOGISISHABRITISHALLIENITALIANATIRETHAIBEN

1. ______________ 2. ______________ 3. ______________

4. ______________ 5. ______________

Ein traditioneller Braten – oft als **roast dinner** bezeichnet, auch wenn er mittags serviert wird – bleibt ganz weit vorn bei den Briten, besonders an Sonn- und Feiertagen. Dass die Franzosen die Briten als **les rosbifs** bezeichnen wird meistens mit einem Schmunzeln akzeptiert, schließlich nennen die Briten ihre gallischen Nachbarn scherzhaft **frogs.**

Roast dinner

Wer *Asterix bei den Briten* gelesen hat, könnte meinen, es wird zu allen Gerichten Pfefferminzsoße serviert. Aber welche Beilagen gehören traditionell wirklich zu welchem Braten?

1. roast beef
2. roast pork
3. roast lamb
4. roast chicken

___ **A** Yorkshire pudding, horseradish sauce

___ **B** stuffing, cranberry sauce, bread sauce

___ **C** apple sauce, crackling

___ **D** mint sauce

Traditional British dishes

Manche Gerichte haben etwas seltsame Namen. Versuchen Sie die Bilder der jeweils passenden Beschreibung zuzuordnen.

1

2

3

4

A **Ploughman's lunch:** This is a cheese salad, often served with chutney. It was traditionally eaten by farm workers.

B **Laverbread:** This is actually not bread at all, but a Welsh speciality made out of seaweed. It is sometimes served as part of a full Welsh breakfast.

C **Bubble and squeak:** This is a side dish made out of fried mashed potato, cabbage and other vegetables. Its name comes from the noises it makes while it is cooking.

D **Toad in the hole:** This dish consists of sausages baked in the kind of batter that is used to make Yorkshire pudding.

Glorious grub

False friends

Manche englische Bezeichnungen sehen deutschen Wörtern zwar ähnlich, haben aber eine ganz andere Bedeutung. Wählen Sie die richtigen Wörter aus.

1. Would you like some strawberry ______________ *(Marmelade)* on your toast?
2. I had a cup of coffee and ______________ *(Kekse)* during the break.
3. My favourite starter is ______________ *(Krabben-)* cocktail.
4. We ordered a vegetarian pizza with red and green ______________ *(Paprika)* on it.

A biscuits **B** crab **C** prawn **D** peppers

E marmalade **F** paprika **G** jam **H** cakes

Sandwich culture

Wie gut kennen Sie die britische Sandwichkultur?

Das **sandwich** wurde nach seinem Erfinder John Montagu, dem IV. Graf von Sandwich (1718–1792) benannt. Er galt als spielsüchtig und unterbrach nur ungern sein geliebtes Cribbage-Kartenspiel. Etwas Fleisch zwischen zwei Brotscheiben konnte er jedoch einfach in der Hand halten, während er weiterspielte. Das **sandwich** wurde dann rasch zum Modesnack der Londoner High Society.

1. Subway and Pret-a-Manger are popular SHINAC ______________ that sell sandwiches.
2. HALMEWOEL ______________ bread is usually healthier than white bread.
3. A DELFIL LOLR ______________ ______________ is a good alternative to a sandwich.
4. Many cafés offer STATODE ______________ sandwiches as a hot snack.
5. A BLUC ______________ sandwich is usually served with salad, crisps or chips.

English breakfast

H	R	F	A	I	N	B	B	A	Y	Z	M	M	S	J
I	E	G	D	E	M	Z	A	I	X	Q	T	P	R	Y
D	N	U	K	X	G	R	K	C	T	H	B	N	O	L
K	K	R	E	D	U	Z	E	Y	O	O	L	B	N	L
V	T	N	P	H	S	T	D	S	M	N	A	S	R	Q
S	G	G	E	D	E	L	B	M	A	R	C	S	B	D
E	M	E	S	N	D	Y	E	I	T	Z	K	E	T	Z
I	I	O	O	T	F	Y	A	Z	O	S	P	A	K	W
B	E	V	O	O	R	A	N	G	E	J	U	I	C	E
D	R	J	K	R	H	Z	S	G	S	R	D	D	F	Z
P	Y	I	I	R	H	L	A	U	J	O	D	D	C	I
A	V	A	X	Q	F	S	M	Z	I	U	I	C	P	K
Y	O	J	S	N	U	R	U	V	C	F	N	G	I	D
R	N	Z	B	A	M	S	Y	M	Y	Q	G	V	Y	G
F	U	Z	S	K	F	U	L	V	P	T	J	D	Y	F

In dem Wortgitter sind neun beliebte Bestandteile eines **full English breakfast** versteckt. Die deutschen unten stehenden Bezeichnungen helfen Ihnen bei der Suche.

Blutwurst

(weiße) Bohnen in Tomatensoße

Tomaten

Champignons

Rühreier

(Schinken-)Speck

Toast

Würstchen

Orangensaft

Heutzutage essen die meisten Briten im Alltag nur ein kleines Frühstück, basierend auf Toast oder Zerealien. Dennoch bleibt die Kalorienbombe namens **full English breakfast** eine beliebte Ausnahme am Wochenende, nach einer durchzechten Nacht oder im Urlaub. Es gibt übrigens auch nicht-englische Varianten, etwa mit **white pudding** (aus Fleisch und Haferflocken) in Irland oder **haggis** (gekochter Schafsmagen gefüllt mit Innereien und Haferschrot) oder **smoked haddock** (geräuchter Schellfisch) in Schottland.

Let’s celebrate!

A Victorian Christmas

Viele der heutigen **Weihnachtsbräuche** in Großbritannien wurden von Königin Victoria und ihrem deutschen Mann, Albert, im 19. Jahrhundert eingeführt, unter anderem der **Weihnachtsbaum, Knallbonbons** und das Verschicken von **Weihnachtskarten**.

Another strange British custom

Der letzte Tag vor der Fastenzeit heißt **Shrove Tuesday**, auch als **Pancake Day** bekannt. Wie andernorts am Mardi Gras und Fasnachtsdienstag nahmen die Leute früher an diesem Tag besonders fettige, reichhaltige Speisen zu sich. Wie sich's gehört, haben die Briten eine skurrile Sportart dazu erfunden: das **Pfannkuchenrennen**.

Let's celebrate!

The fifth of November

Jedes Jahr am 5. November wird **Bonfire Night**, auch als **Guy Fawkes Night** bekannt, gefeiert. Was wissen Sie über diese britische Tradition?

The famous Gunpowder Plot took place in the year 1605. A group of **1.** ______________ planned to blow up the English Parliament and kill the **2.** ______________ (James I). They were angry because their **3.** ______________ was not accepted by the Protestant **4.** ______________. One of the men, Guy Fawkes, hid **5.** ______________ in the cellar of the Houses of Parliament but these were discovered in the early hours of 5th November. The king and parliament were saved. On this date every **6.** ______________, people celebrate this historic event by lighting large **7.** ______________, watching spectacular **8.** ______________ and burning a 'guy', a model of Guy Fawkes.

A religion B year C explosives D firework displays

E king F Catholics G aristocracy H bonfires

Celebrations

Welches Bild passt zu welchem Fest?

1

2

3

4

A Halloween

B Valentine's Day

C Easter

D Christmas

Gesetzliche Feiertage heißen **bank holidays** (ursprünglich, weil die Banken an diesen Tagen geschlossen waren). Neben kirchlichen Feiertagen in der Oster- und Weihnachtszeit sind in England und Wales auch der erste und letzte Montag im Mai sowie der letzte Montag im August für viele arbeits- und schulfrei. In Schottland und Irland gibt es teilweise andere Regelungen.

Celebrating differently

Manche Feste werden in Großbritannien anders gefeiert. Wie gut kennen Sie sich aus?

1. On which day is Christmas celebrated?

☐ **A** 24th December
☐ **B** 25th December
☐ **C** 26th December

2. Which is a bank holiday?

☐ **A** Good Friday *(Karfreitag)*
☐ **B** Labour Day *(Tag der Arbeit)*
☐ **C** All Saints' Day *(Allerheiligen)*

3. What do people call the 26th of December?

☐ **A** Christmas Eve
☐ **B** New Year's Day
☐ **C** Boxing Day

4. Which of these is celebrated on different days in Germany and Britain?

☐ **A** Mother's Day
☐ **B** Easter
☐ **C** Halloween

Traditions and superstitions

Aberglaube und alte Traditionen prägen nach wie vor manche Bräuche. Können Sie die fehlenden Wörter einfügen?

1. At Christmas, people kiss under the ____________.

2. Children are told that Father Christmas comes down the ____________.

3. For good luck, a bride should wear "something old, something new, something borrowed, something ____________".

4. British people often say "Touch ____________!" when they wish something good to come true.

5. On April Fool's Day (1 April) people play ____________ on each other.

A tricks **B** wood **C** mistletoe **D** blue **E** chimney

Let's celebrate!

Party small talk

Feste und Feiern bieten gute Gelegenheiten, miteinander ins Gespräch zu kommen. Ergänzen Sie die Floskeln.

1. You have given someone a gift on their birthday and they have thanked you. How do you reply?
   - ☐ **A** No thanks.
   - ☐ **B** Please.
   - ☐ **C** You're welcome.
   - ☐ **D** It's nothing.

2. Which is correct? "Congratulations ... your birthday / retirement / wedding."
   - ☐ **A** to
   - ☐ **B** on
   - ☐ **C** for
   - ☐ **D** about

3. You would like to ask someone to go on a date with you: "Would you like to go ... with me?"
   - ☐ **A** away
   - ☐ **B** off
   - ☐ **C** out
   - ☐ **D** around

4. You have enjoyed talking to someone: "It's been ... talking to you."
   - ☐ **A** fun
   - ☐ **B** funny
   - ☐ **C** OK
   - ☐ **D** amusing

Reasons to celebrate

Welches Wort passt zu welchem Anlass?

1. Someone is finishing work because of their age.
2. Two people are getting married at this event.
3. A baby is being baptized in a church.
4. This is when two people decide they want to get married.
5. Someone has successfully finished their university course.

___ **A** christening

___ **B** graduation

___ **C** engagement

___ **D** retirement

___ **E** wedding

Welche vier Aussagen treffen auf Großbritannien zu und welche nicht?

Celebration customs

	YES	NO
1. Sometimes people say "Happy Birthday" before the actual birthday.	☐	☐
2. It is OK to give someone flowers wrapped in paper or plastic.	☐	☐
3. The average person in Britain sends 50 Christmas cards every year.	☐	☐
4. If an invitation says "7.30 pm for 8", you should arrive by 7.30 pm.	☐	☐
5. If it is your birthday, you should buy everyone a drink.	☐	☐
6. Housewarming parties are always held during cold weather.	☐	☐
7. It is not very polite to talk about how much you earn during small talk.	☐	☐
8. At a party, you should immediately introduce yourself to all the other guests.	☐	☐

Wedding traditions

Welches Bild zeigt eine Hochzeitstradition, die in Großbritannien und Irland eher unbekannt ist?

1

2

3

4

Politics and news media

British politics

Welche Antwort stimmt?

1. The prime minister lives at house number 10 of which street?
   - ☐ A Baker Street
   - ☐ B Oxford Street
   - ☐ C Downing Street

2. Which part of parliament used to be open to aristocrats only and is sometimes called "the upper house"?
   - ☐ A the House of Lords
   - ☐ B the Cabinet
   - ☐ C the House of Commons

3. Which Cabinet member is equivalent to the German *Außenminister(in)*?
   - ☐ A foreign secretary
   - ☐ B home secretary
   - ☐ C health secretary

4. Which of the three biggest political parties has red as its colour?
   - ☐ A Conservatives
   - ☐ B Labour
   - ☐ C Liberal Democrats

Elections and parliament

Ergänzen Sie den Text über das Wahlsystem in Großbritannien.

The **1.** ____________ of the UK elect **2.** ____________ of Parliament (MPs) to the House of **3.** ____________ every five **4.** ____________. Most MPs belong to a political party, and the party that wins the most **5.** ____________ forms the **6.** ____________ – this method of counting votes is known as the 'first-past-the-post system'. The prime **7.** ____________ leads the government. New **8.** ____________ have to be approved by the House of Commons and the House of Lords.

A seats	B years	C government	D people
E Members	F Commons	G laws	H minister

Seit den späten 1990er Jahren gibt es auch Regionalparlamente in Schottland, Wales und Nordirland, die auf bestimmten Gebieten – wie Bildung, Gesundheitswesen und Kulturpolitik – gesetzgebende Befugnisse für die jeweilige Region besitzen. Andere Bereiche – wie Verteidigung, Einwanderung und Außenpolitik – bleiben jedoch dem britischen Parlament vorbehalten.

Prime ministers

Können Sie die Namen dieser berühmten britischen Premierminister herausfinden?

Während des 2. Weltkriegs wurde der Spruch **„V for victory“** und das Handzeichen dazu vom damaligen Premierminister **Winston Churchill** berühmt gemacht. Heutzutage gilt diese Geste sowohl als Friedenszeichen als auch für die Zahl 2. Aber Vorsicht, denn mit dem Handrücken nach vorne gehalten ist diese Geste gleichbedeutend mit einem „Stinkefinger“.

1. This politician was a member of the government during both world wars and won the Nobel Prize for Literature in 1953.
   SWONNIT CHILCHURL ____________ ____________

2. Britain's longest serving and only female prime minister (1979–1990). Many people remember her fights with the EU and her strong will, which earned her the name "Iron Lady".
   GRAMTREA RHACHETT ____________ ____________

3. This prime minister was criticised for taking Britain into the Iraq War in 2003. His government also set up regional parliaments for Scotland, Wales and Northern Ireland.
   YONT LIBRA ____________ ____________

More about British politics

Welche Satzteile gehören zusammen?

1. Most members of the Cabinet
2. Many members of the House of Lords
3. Only members of the House of Commons
4. All new laws
5. The regional parliaments in Wales and Northern Ireland

__ **A** have to be signed by the monarch.

__ **B** do not belong to a political party.

__ **C** are the heads of government departments.

__ **D** are actually called assemblies.

__ **E** are called Members of Parliament (MPs).

Politics and news media

Newspaper culture

Neben der seriösen Presse, **broadsheets** oder **quality press** genannt, gibt es in Großbritannien eine berühmtberüchtigte Boulevardpresse, vertreten durch die so genannte **tabloid press** (oder abwertender: **gutter press**). Der veraltete amerikanische Begriff **yellow press** wird in Großbritannien übrigens nicht verwendet.

Welche der unten stehenden Begriffe gehören zu welchem Typ Zeitung?

1. broadsheet: ____________________
2. tabloid: ____________________

A sensational B big headlines

C serious D scandals

E lots of pictures F informative

G in-depth news

H celebrity gossip

I horoscopes

J more intellectual

Other news media

Welches Wort ist richtig?

1. The important news media companies have their own internet **sites / sides**.
2. Very important news that has just come in is sometimes called **breaking / broken** news.
3. Many people read online **blogs / blocks** as well as print media.
4. The news on TV or radio is presented by a **newsreader / public speaker**.
5. A lot of journalists and **politics / politicians** use social media such as Twitter to share their ideas.
6. You can listen to BBC radio all over the world because they **broadcast / send** their programmes online.

Achtung: Ein Laden, der Zeitungen und Zeitschriften verkauft, heißt **newsagent's (shop)**; die großen Nachrichtenagenturen (wie z. B. Reuters, AP und die DPA) sind dagegen **news agencies**.

News and politics

Welcher Begriff passt am besten zum Bild?

1

- ☐ **A** title
- ☐ **B** headline
- ☐ **C** link
- ☐ **D** programme

2

- ☐ **A** Cabinet
- ☐ **B** MP
- ☐ **C** election
- ☐ **D** political party

3

- ☐ **A** news conference
- ☐ **B** newsflash
- ☐ **C** news magazine
- ☐ **D** news agency

British newspapers

Finden Sie die Namen sechs bekannter britischer Zeitungen (jeweils ohne „the") und markieren Sie diese mit „B" für **broadsheet** oder „T" für **tabloid.**

CARMIRRORENDETIMESSETGUARDIANOSUNILENTELEGRAPHEMEDAILYMAILMAN

1. ____________________ 2. ____________________

3. ____________________ 4. ____________________

5. ____________________ 6. ____________________

Shakespeare's country

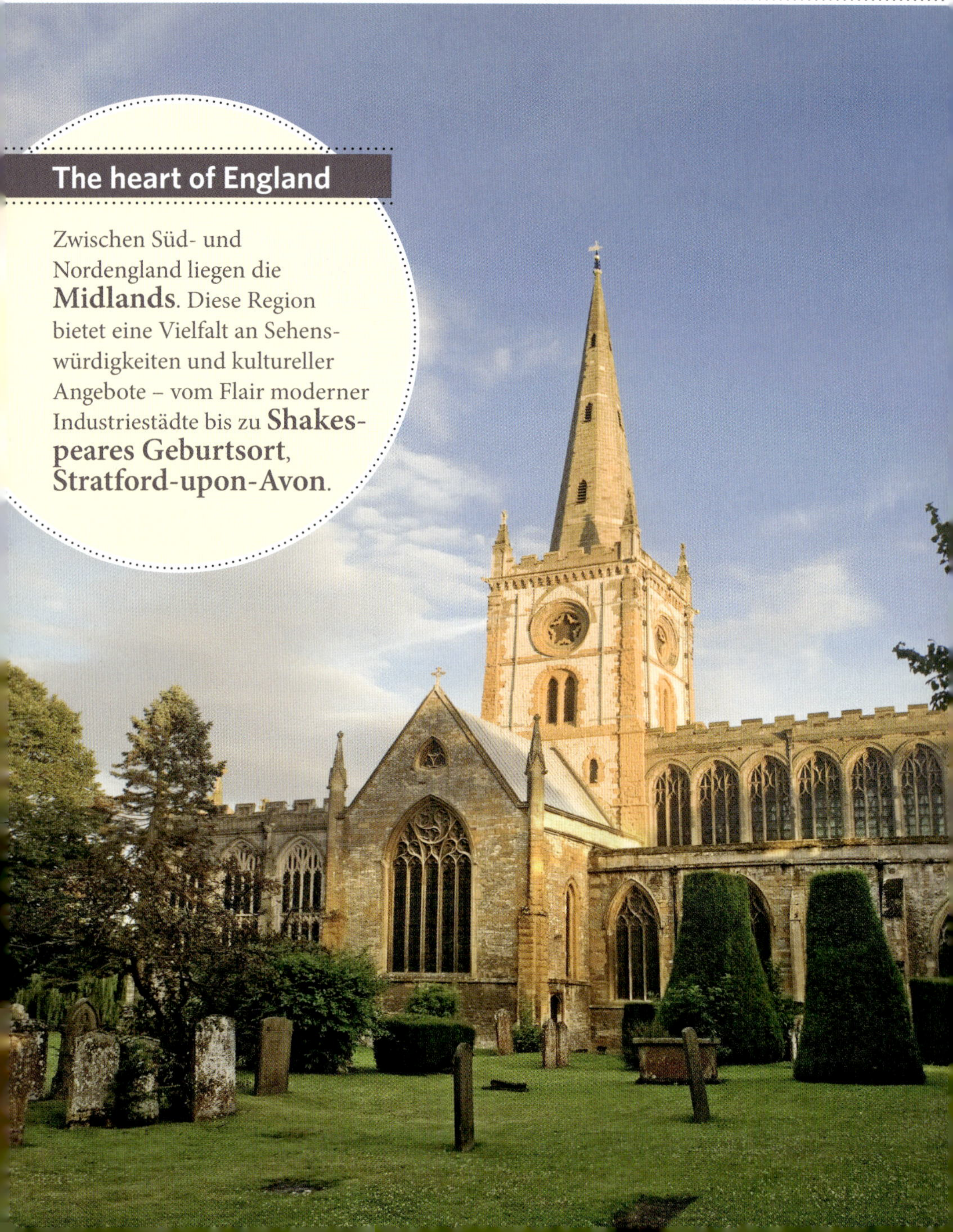

The heart of England

Zwischen Süd- und Nordengland liegen die **Midlands**. Diese Region bietet eine Vielfalt an Sehenswürdigkeiten und kultureller Angebote – vom Flair moderner Industriestädte bis zu **Shakespeares Geburtsort, Stratford-upon-Avon**.

Industrial heritage

Westlich von **Birmingham** kann man das UNESCO-Weltkulturerbe **Ironbridge Gorge** besuchen. Die erste gusseiserne Bogenbrücke der Welt wurde hier **1779** von **Thomas Telford** über den Fluss Severn gebaut. **Ironbridge** mit seinen Museen bildet heute einen Ankerpunkt der Europäischen Route der Industriekultur (ERIH), dem touristischen Informationsnetzwerk zum industriellen Erbe in Europa.

Shakespeare's country

Birmingham

Vervollständigen Sie die Sätze mit dem jeweils passenden Wort.

Der Begriff **Midlands** ist nicht gleichbedeutend mit **Middle England**: Letzterer kommt aus der Politik und bezieht sich eher abstrakt auf den konservativen Mittelstand Englands.

With six million trees and more **1.** ______________ than any other European city, Birmingham is certainly green. It also has more **2.** ______________ than Venice: there are 56km of waterways in the city. It is the UK's largest manufacturing centre and produces 25% of UK **3.** ______________. In the past it was known as 'the city of 1,000 **4.** ______________' – these included the manufacture of guns, jewellery and pens. Today Birmingham houses more than 500,000 **5.** ______________ of art within one city centre square mile and the world's largest collection of rock album **6.** ______________ can be visited at St Paul's Gallery in the Jewellery Quarter. Birmingham has over 100 **7.** ______________ specialising in Balti cuisine, a spicy Kashmiri style of cooking. A third of the city's **8.** ______________ are of ethnic minority origin.

A covers **B** trades **C** canals **D** restaurants

E parks **F** exports **G** works **H** residents

Other towns and cities

Welches Bild passt zu welcher Stadt?

1

2

3

4

___ **A** Rugby ___ **B** Leamington Spa ___ **C** Stratford-upon-Avon

___ **D** Nottingham

The Midlands

Was gibt es in den Midlands sonst noch zu sehen?

1

- ☐ A Alton Towers Resort
- ☐ B Royal Shakespeare Theatre
- ☐ C Twycross Zoo

2

- ☐ A National Motorcycle Museum
- ☐ B Warwick Castle
- ☐ C National Space Centre

3

- ☐ A Cadbury World
- ☐ B Chatsworth House
- ☐ C Coventry Cathedral

4

- ☐ A Acton Scott Historic Working Farm
- ☐ B Buxton Pavilion Gardens
- ☐ C Silverstone Racing Circuit

The industrial past and present

Verbinden Sie die Satzteile.

1. The Black Country west of Birmingham ___
2. Jaguar and Daimler ___
3. The area of Staffordshire that is known as "The Potteries" ___
4. The crisp manufacturer Walkers ___
5. Northampton's shoemaking industry ___

A uses 280,000 tonnes of potatoes every year at its huge East Midlands factory.

B has supplied footwear for several James Bond films.

C got its name from the soot and smoke produced by heavy industry in the area.

D are car manufacturers with historical links to the city of Coventry.

E still produces well-known brands such as Wedgewood.

Shakespeare's country

Robin Hood

Robin Hood gilt als Sohn der Midlands. Was wissen Sie über ihn?

Die **Robin-Hood-**Statue mitten in **Nottingham** ist nur eins von vielen Beispielen, wie die Legende zelebriert wird. Die Stadt hat aber noch mehr zu bieten, wie z. B uralte Kneipen, eine mittelalterliche Burg und einige überregional wichtige Sportanlagen.

1. What is the name of the forest where Robin Hood lived?

☐ A Sherwood Forest ☐ B Black Forest ☐ C Forrest Gump

2. Who was Robin's greatest enemy?

☐ A the Duke of York ☐ B the Sheriff of Nottingham
☐ C the Mayor of London

3. What was the name of Robin's female companion?

☐ A Guinevere ☐ B Hermione ☐ C Marian

4. Robin and his men "stole from the rich to give to the ...".

☐ A poor ☐ B dead ☐ C birds

5. Which of these was **not** one of Robin's men?

☐ A Friar Tuck ☐ B Little John ☐ C Bilbo Baggins

Midlands specialities

Welche nach Ortsnamen benannten Spezialitäten sind hier zu sehen?

A Stilton cheese

B Bakewell tart

C Lincolnshire sausages

D Melton Mowbray pork pie

Shakespeares Person ist von vielen Mythen umgeben, aber nur drei dieser Aussagen stimmen **nicht**. Können Sie sie finden?

Shakespeare's life and works

- ☐ **1.** Shakespeare's birthday and day of death were the same (23 April).
- ☐ **2.** He worked as an actor for much of his life.
- ☐ **3.** Shakespeare's son was called Hamlet.
- ☐ **4.** There is no evidence for him writing his name as "Shakespeare".
- ☐ **5.** All female theatre roles had to be played by men during Shakespeare's lifetime.
- ☐ **6.** Two of Shakespeare's plays have been translated into Klingon, a *Star Trek* language.
- ☐ **7.** Shakespeare's works use more than 30,000 different words.
- ☐ **8.** He had a very good university education.
- ☐ **9.** Some people believe that other people wrote his plays.
- ☐ **10.** Shakespeare stayed in Stratford-upon-Avon all his life.

Es steht aber außer Frage, dass **William Shakespeare** weltweit der am häufigsten zitierte Autor überhaupt ist. Darüber hinaus gibt es über 2.000 Wörter im Englischen, die vor seinen Werken nirgendwo geschrieben standen (z. B. **critical, excellent, countless**).

Shakespeare quotations

Können Sie diese bekannten Shakespeare-Zitate ergänzen?

A stage

B love

C music

D winter

E question

1. "If ________ be the food of love, play on." *(Twelfth Night)*
2. "All the world's a ________, and all the men and women merely players." *(As You Like It)*
3. "To be, or not to be: that is the ________." *(Hamlet)*
4. "The course of true ________ never did run smooth." *(A Midsummer Night's Dream)*
5. "Now is the ________ of our discontent." *(Richard III)*

On screen: TV and film

British TV and film

Das Wort **screen** bezeichnet sowohl die „Kinoleinwand“ (**cinema screen** oder etwas poetischer **silver screen**) als auch einen „Bildschirm“ (z. B. **TV screen** oder **computer screen**). Weitere Bedeutungen sind „Blende“, „Sichtschirm“ und „Schutz“ (z. B. **sunscreen** für „Sonnencreme“).

Welche Satzteile gehören zusammen?

1. Alfred Hitchcock and David Lean
2. ITV, Channel 4 and Sky
3. Harry Potter and James Bond
4. The annual BAFTA awards
5. In 2009, British films
6. The *Doctor Who* BBC series

___ **A** are Britain's best known commercial TV broadcasting stations.

___ **B** are Britain's equivalent of the Oscars.

___ **C** is the longest-running science fiction TV show in the world.

___ **D** had a 7% share of the global market.

___ **E** are two of the most famous film directors of all time.

___ **F** are the world's highest-earning film franchises.

History of the BBC

Vervollständigen Sie den Text mit dem jeweils richtigen Wort.

The British Broadcasting Corporation was **1.** ______________ in 1922. About 23,000 people are **2.** ______________ by the BBC, and it is **3.** ______________ to be the world's largest broadcasting company. It is mainly **4.** ______________ by a licence fee system. The BBC operates a number of TV channels and radio stations, and it is **5.** ______________ for its news programmes. It is still **6.** ______________ on its original aim "to inform, educate and entertain". Its broadcast of the 2012 Olympics Opening Ceremony was **7.** ______________ by 27.3 million people in Britain alone. The BBC is sometimes **8.** ______________ "the Beeb".

A well-known	**B** watched	**C** employed	**D** financed
E believed	**F** called	**G** founded	**H** focused

Murder mysteries and thrillers

Ob im Fernsehen, im Kino oder als Lektüre – die Briten lieben Krimis. Wissen Sie, wer diese bekannten Krimifiguren kreiert hat?

1. Miss Marple
2. Sherlock Holmes
3. Inspector Morse
4. James Bond
5. Inspector Lynley

___ **A** Elizabeth George

___ **B** Colin Dexter

___ **C** Ian Fleming

___ **D** Arthur Conan Doyle

___ **E** Agatha Christie

Sherlock Holmes gilt laut dem *Guinness Buch der Rekorde* als die am häufigsten auf der Leinwand gezeigte Romanfigur – bis anno 2012 waren es 254 Verfilmungen mit über 75 Schauspielern in dieser Rolle.

British films

Können Sie die Beschreibungen dem jeweils richtigen Filmtitel zuordnen?

1. In this thriller set in Vienna, an American writer investigates the mysterious death of his friend Harry Lime. He discovers a complex network of criminal activity.
2. In this comedy drama, a group of steel workers lose their jobs. As they are desperate to earn money, they decide to become strippers.
3. This drama is set around the time of World War II and tells the story of a man who has been badly burned. He is looked after by a French-Canadian nurse in an Italian monastery.
4. This comedy film tells the story of a young man who is born the same night and on the same street as Jesus Christ.
5. An English man, Charles, and an American woman, Carrie, meet when friends get married. They have a very complicated love affair.

___ **A** *Four Weddings and a Funeral*

___ **B** *Life of Brian*

___ **C** *The English Patient*

___ **D** *The Third Man*

___ **E** *The Full Monty*

On screen: TV and film

Film and TV vocabulary

Welche Antwort ist richtig?

1. We really want to see the play – all the newspapers have written good ... of it.
   - ☐ **A** articles
   - ☐ **B** critics
   - ☐ **C** reviews

2. BBC1 and BBC2 are two of the best TV ... in Britain.
   - ☐ **A** channels
   - ☐ **B** companies
   - ☐ **C** senders

3. The talk show presenter asked the studio ... for their opinion.
   - ☐ **A** audience
   - ☐ **B** population
   - ☐ **C** public

4. The ... we booked for the film were quite good, even though they were cheap.
   - ☐ **A** chairs
   - ☐ **B** places
   - ☐ **C** seats

5. We watched a fascinating nature ... on TV last night.
   - ☐ **A** documentary
   - ☐ **B** document
   - ☐ **C** documentation

6. Oliver Stone is a world-famous film ... .
   - ☐ **A** conductor
   - ☐ **B** director
   - ☐ **C** register

Different genres

Versteckt sind fünf Wörter, die oft benutzt werden, um verschiedene Genres zu bezeichnen. Können Sie sie finden?

BARACTIONANYADVENTUREDVERSTRAGEDYSTHRILLERINGEFANTASYLLODE

1. ______________________ 2. ______________________

3. ______________________ 4. ______________________

5. ______________________

Obwohl **James Bond** weltweit als typisch englische Filmfigur gilt, wurde die Rolle größtenteils von Nicht-Engländern gespielt. Der Schotte Sean Connery gilt vielen als der perfekte Bond-Darsteller, aber auch der Waliser Timothy Dalton, der Ire Pierce Brosnan und der Australier George Lazenby spielten diese heiß begehrte Rolle.

Bond, James Bond

Können Sie mit Hilfe der Bilder die Titel dieser James Bond-Filme ergänzen?

1

1. *From SIRASU* ______ *With Love* (1963)

2

2. *MAINDODS* ______ *Are Forever* (1971)

3

3. *MOTORWOR* ______ *Never Dies* (1997)

4

4. *SACION* ______ *Royale* (2006)

British Oscar winners

Wer hat für welchen Film einen Oscar in der Kategorie **Best Actor / Actress** gewonnen?

1. *Gone With the Wind* (1939)
2. *Hamlet* (1948)
3. *Mary Poppins* (1964)
4. *Gandhi* (1982)
5. *The Silence of the Lambs* (1991)
6. *The Queen* (2006)
7. *The Reader* (2008)
8. *The King's Speech* (2010)

___ A Julie Andrews
___ B Colin Firth
___ C Helen Mirren
___ D Ben Kingsley
___ E Laurence Olivier
___ F Anthony Hopkins
___ G Vivien Leigh
___ H Kate Winslet

The Emerald Isle

Ancient natural landscapes

Wegen seiner vielerorts **smaragdgrünen Landschaft** wird Irland auch **Emerald Isle** genannt. Dieses Bild zeigt die **Cliffs of Moher** an der Südwestküste in County Clare. Geschätzte **30.000 Vögel**, etwa 30 unterschiedlicher Arten, leben in diesen uralten Klippen.

Symbols of Ireland

Der **leprechaun**, ein zwergenhaftes mythologisches Wesen, gehört neben der **harp** (Harfe), dem **shamrock** (Kleeblatt) und dem **keltischen Kreuz** zu den Wahrzeichen Irlands. Dargestellt wird dieser Kobold meistens in grüner Kleidung mit rotem Haar und Bart.

The Emerald Isle

Ireland's main cities

Welche Beschreibung passt zu welcher Stadt?

1. Belfast **2.** Dublin **3.** Cork

4. Limerick **5.** Galway

___ **A** This medieval city lies where the River Shannon enters the Atlantic.

___ **B** This is the capital of Northern Ireland and the Titanic was built here.

___ **C** Located in the South West, this city has two cathedrals.

___ **D** This is the capital of the Republic of Ireland and was home to writer James Joyce.

___ **E** In the West of Ireland, this city is known for its many arts and music festivals.

The economy of Ireland

Wählen Sie das jeweils richtige Wort aus.

The Republic of Ireland used to be one of the poorest **1.** ________________ of the European **2.** ________________, but from the 1990s to 2007 it experienced an economic **3.** ________________ that made it rich and successful.

The country's **4.** ________________ worked with employers to improve the situation, there was **5.** ________________ by foreign companies, low **6.** ________________ helped businesses, and the EU provided financial support. Because of its economic strength, Ireland became known as the "Celtic **7.** ________________", even though it has been hit by **8.** ________________ since that time.

A boom **B** Tiger **C** Union **D** investment

E recession **F** tax rates **G** members **H** government

The Republic of Ireland

In Irland ist einiges anders.
Verbinden Sie die Satzteile richtig.

Wie alle offiziellen Dokumente ist der irische Pass zweisprachig – zuerst kommt die Information auf Irisch, dann auf Englisch.

1. The currency used
2. The Church of Ireland
3. The head of state
4. The English language
5. The Irish national flag

___ **A** is the second official language (Irish is the first).

___ **B** is the president, not the British monarch.

___ **C** is not the pound sterling but the euro.

___ **D** is Catholic, not Protestant.

___ **E** is green, white and orange.

The road to peace

Bringen Sie die Ereignisse zum Frieden in Nordirland in die richtige chronologische Reihenfolge.

___ **A** In the 1990s the two sides agreed to stop fighting and held peace talks, leading to the Good Friday Agreement in 1998.

___ **B** The British army was called in to take control from the police, but a few years later in 1972 they killed 14 people at a peaceful demonstration.

___ **C** Since 1999 the problems have not gone away but are much more under control.

___ **D** In 1968 police attacked people who were campaigning for Catholics' rights.

___ **E** The Northern Ireland Assembly took over political control in 1999.

___ **F** The Irish Republican Army (IRA) reacted by attacking British targets, and this went on into the 1980s. There were also terrorist groups on the Protestant side.

The Emerald Isle

Places to visit

Welche Beschreibung passt zu welchem Bild?

A The library here has over a million books and manuscripts, including the world-famous *Book of Kells*.

B This pretty fishing village in County Cork attracts tourists with its marina, art galleries and restaurants.

C This prehistoric monument in County Meath is older than Stonehenge but also had astronomical significance.

D These strange rock formations in County Antrim, Northern Ireland, are the result of volcanic activity.

1

Newgrange

2

Kinsale

3

Giant's Causeway

4

Dublin Trinity College

Famous Irish artists

Wofür sind diese irischen Künstler bekannt?

1. Bob Geldof
2. Liam Neeson
3. George Bernard Shaw
4. Niamh Cusack
5. Sinéad O'Connor

___ A This actress is a member of a well-known acting family: her sisters Sinéad and Sorcha are also famous.

___ B He won an Oscar and the Nobel Prize in Literature for the play *Pygmalion*.

___ C This actor has starred in films including *Schindler's List*, *Love Actually* and *Michael Collins*.

___ D This female singer-songwriter is probably best known for the song "Nothing Compares to You".

___ E He was the singer for the Boomtown Rats and is also known for his political activism and charity work.

Aufgrund großer Auswanderungswellen, insbesondere im 19. und 20. Jahrhundert, leben heute weltweit Millionen Menschen irischer Herkunft. Man denke z. B. an den **Kennedy-Clan** in den USA oder an die internationale Beliebtheit des **St Patrick's Day**.

Irish English

Einige Wörter sind im irischen Englisch anders. Finden Sie die passende britische Bezeichnung für das jeweils fett gedruckte Wort.

1. I need to buy new **runners** so that I can go jogging without hurting my feet.
   ☐ **A** gloves ☐ **B** shorts ☐ **C** trainers

2. There's been a robbery! Quick, someone must call the **gardai**!
   ☐ **A** ambulance ☐ **B** fire brigade ☐ **C** police

3. What a fantastic evening that was – it was really great **craic**!
   ☐ **A** disappointment ☐ **B** fun ☐ **C** disaster

4. I don't drink alcohol. Will there be **minerals** as well as alcoholic drinks available?
   ☐ **A** soft drinks ☐ **B** spirits ☐ **C** wines

5. Please put the plates away in the **press** when you have washed and dried them.
   ☐ **A** cupboard ☐ **B** dishwasher ☐ **C** dustbin

Guinness

Guinness: one of the world's most popular beer brands. Bringen Sie die Buchstaben der fehlenden Wörter in die richtige Reihenfolge.

1. Arthur Guinness set up his first YERWERB ____________ in Leixlip in 1756.
2. Today Guinness is brewed in over 150 ERITCUNOS ____________, including Nigeria and Indonesia.
3. The Guinness Storehouse in Dublin is one of Ireland's top tourist TACTRANOSIT ____________.
4. Over ten million SLEGASS ____________ of Guinness are sold worldwide every day.
5. Much more is sold on St TAKPCIR ____________'s Day (17 March), the Irish holiday that is celebrated internationally.
6. Pouring the perfect pint of Guinness takes time – ideally 199.50 ENDOSCS ____________.

Music and art in Britain

British bands

ACROASISTERLYTHEPOLICELLULLEDZEPPELINGATHESMITHSONICOLDPLAYTIME

Britpop war eine alternative Rockmusikbewegung, die Anfang der 1990er Jahre entstand. Beeinflusst durch ältere britische Bands wie die **Beatles, Rolling Stones** und **Stone Roses,** verstand sich **Britpop** mit seinen oft lyrischen, eher gitarrenlastigen Songs als Gegenströmung zum amerikanischen **Grunge.**

Finden Sie die Namen fünf bekannter britischer Bands in der Wortschlange? Die Hinweise unten helfen Ihnen sie zu finden.

1. This rock band was formed in 1964 by Robert Plant, Jimmy Page and others, and their greatest hit was probably "Stairway to Heaven". ____________
2. This band mixed punk, reggae and jazz in the late 1970s and 1980s. The lead singer, Sting, later started a successful solo career. ____________
3. This 1980s alternative rock band had Morrissey as its lead singer and was known for its rather melancholy songs such as "Heaven Knows I'm Missing You Now". ____________
4. This Manchester Britpop band included brothers Liam and Noel Gallagher. Their second album *(What's the Story) Morning Glory?* made them world-famous. ____________
5. This group played a major role in the closing ceremony of the 2012 London Olympics. Its lead singer, Chris Martin, was married to actress Gwyneth Paltrow. ____________

Music & Co

Können Sie diese berühmten Namen mit der richtigen Beschreibung verbinden?

1. The London recording studio that was made famous by the Beatles.
2. A British record label founded by the entrepreneur Richard Branson, who also owns an airline with the same name.
3. This record label was founded by the Beatles. A world-famous computer company has the same name.
4. A Manchester nightclub that used to be known as "the most famous club in the world".

___ **A** The Hacienda

___ **B** Abbey Road

___ **C** Virgin

___ **D** Apple

Diese Bilder zeigen Motive, die jeweils zu einem von Andrew Lloyd Webbers Musicals passen. Wie gut kennen Sie sich damit aus?

A *Evita* B *Cats* C *Phantom of the Opera* D *Starlight Express*

Andrew Lloyd Webber

Andrew Lloyd Webber (geb. 1948) ist der erfolgreichste Musicalkomponist unserer Zeit. Mehrere seiner zahlreichen Musicals liefen über Jahrzehnte im Londoner West End und am Broadway in New York, aber auch jenseits der Bühne belegten Songs wie „Don't Cry for me Argentina" *(Evita)* oder „Memory" *(Cats)* die oberen Plätze in den internationalen Hitparaden.

Wer ist wofür bekannt?

British composers

1. His best known work is the 1972 album *Tubular Bells*, written when he was still a teenager.
2. Often seen as a typically English composer, his most famous work is the *Enigma Variations* (1899).
3. This Baroque composer is best known for the opera *Dido and Aeneas.*
4. This composer has provided music for films such as *Prospero's Books* (1991) and *The Piano* (1993).

___ A Edward Elgar (1857–1934) ___ B Michael Nyman (born 1944)

___ C Mike Oldfield (born 1953) ___ D Henry Purcell (1659–1695)

Music and art in Britain

Tate Modern

Vervollständigen Sie den Text mit dem jeweils richtigen Wort.

Tate Modern in London is located in a rather **1.** ____________ building for an art gallery: a **2.** ____________ power station. Today it houses a collection of works by the most important and **3.** ____________ international contemporary artists. There are four permanent exhibitions as well as numerous **4.** ____________ ones. The **5.** ____________ displays using multimedia make the experience varied and **6.** ____________ for visitors. Tate Modern is not only the **7.** ____________ modern art gallery in the world, but it is also the most **8.** ____________: around 4.7 million people pass through its doors every year.

A temporary
B lively
C interactive
D former
E largest
F unusual
G visited
H influential

British artists

Können Sie die Satzteile einander zuordnen?

1. Dante Gabriel Rossetti (1828–1882) was one of
2. David Hockney (born 1937) became known for
3. Tracy Emin (born 1963) is considered one of
4. J. M. W. Turner (1775–1851) is often known as

___ **A** his paintings of swimming pools but he has also used electronic media such as fax machines and apps to create art in recent years.

___ **B** the *enfants terribles* of the Britart movement and is best known for her installation of an unmade bed.

___ **C** "the painter of light" and his Romantic works share features with Impressionism. An important UK art prize is named after him.

___ **D** the founders of the Pre-Raphaelite movement. He was obsessed with the poet Dante and his sister, Christina, was a poet.

Music and art

Hier können Sie Ihre Kenntnisse über die britische Kunst- und Musikszene auf die Probe stellen.

ACROSS →

2. There are 732 portraits of the ... in the National Portrait Gallery.
4. The Royal ... Hall is London's most famous concert hall and is also used for boxing matches.
8. The annual "Last Night of the ..." is Britain's most popular concert and is broadcasted on TV and radio.
9. The artist Damien ... became famous for displaying dead animals in formaldehyde.

DOWN ↓

1. This singer's album *21* became the best-selling album of the 21st century in 2011.
3. No one knows the real identity of this world-famous street artist.
5. A music band which first became famous at the Cavern Club in Liverpool.
6. Sir Simon ... is one of Britain's best known conductors.
7. British painter Lucien ... was the grandson of a world-famous psychoanalyst.

Lösungen

Welcome to Britain!

S. 8

Basic geography
1. C, **2.** A, **3.** E, **4.** B, **5.** D
Great Britain: A, C, E
United Kingdom: A, B, C, E
Ireland: B, D
British Isles: A, B, C, D, E

British history
1. E, **2.** D, **3.** B, **4.** C, **5.** A

S. 9

Top Ten Greatest Britons
1. H, **2.** A, **3.** I, **4.** G, **5.** J, **6.** C, **7.** F, **8.** B, **9.** E, **10.** D

British money
1. E, **2.** G, **3.** B, **4.** F, **5.** C, **6.** H, **7.** A, **8.** D

Das L-förmige Pfundsymbol (**£**) geht auf das lateinische Wort für Pfund, *libra*, zurück. In früheren Zeiten entsprach der Geldwert eines Pfunds dem eines Pfunds Silber, daher auch die offizielle Bezeichnung **pound sterling**. Ein **pound** besteht aus 100 **pence** (**p**).

S. 10

Hello and goodbye
1. D, **2.** B, **3.** B, **4.** C, **5.** D, **6.** A

S. 11

Flags of the UK
1. C, **2.** D, **3.** A, **4.** B

National symbols
1. dragon, **2.** thistle, **3.** unicorn, **4.** oak tree, **5.** harp **6.** lion

This sceptred isle

S. 12

Invaders and conquerors
1. D; **2.** B; **3.** C, E; **4.** A

S. 13

Stories of the sea
1. B *Robinson Crusoe*
2. A *Treasure Island*
3. D *Lord of the Flies*
4. C *Gulliver's Travels*

Dressing for the weather
1. Wellingtons, **2.** umbrella, **3.** trenchcoat, **4.** gloves

S. 14

Weather idioms
1. D, **2.** B, **3.** C, **4.** A, **5.** C, **6.** B
Mögliche Übersetzungen:
1. Das ist ein Sturm im Wasserglas.
2. Es gießt wie aus Kübeln.
3. Ich bin etwas angeschlagen / nicht ganz auf der Höhe.
4. Dieser Nebel ist übel dicht.
5. Jedes Unglück hat auch etwas Gutes.
6. Er nahm die Nachricht mit finsterer Miene auf.

S. 15

Arriving in Britain
Waagrecht: 3. Gatwick, **6.** airport, **11.** Waterloo, **13.** Eurostar, **14.** Manchester, **15.** customs, **16.** railway
Senkrecht: 1. coach, **2.** ferry, **4.** Arrivals, **5.** shuttle, **7.** Eurotunnel, **8.** Stansted, **9.** Heathrow, **10.** passport, **12.** Dover

Das allererste **crossword** in der heute bekannten Form erschien zwar 1913 in einer amerikanischen Zeitung, wurde aber ursprünglich von einem britischen Journalisten aus Liverpool, namens **Arthur Wynne**, erfunden. Fast alle britischen Tageszeitungen enthalten bis heute ein oder zwei Kreuzworträtsel.

London: a nation, not a city

S. 18

London facts
1. C, **2.** C, **3.** B, **4.** D, **5.** A

Travelling on the Tube
1. C, **2.** D, **3.** E, **4.** A, **5.** B

Fahrkarten für die U-Bahn kauft man am Schalter oder am Automaten – weder am Gleis noch im Zug selbst gibt es eine Möglichkeit Fahrkarten zu kaufen. Beachten Sie auch die Angebote für günstige Tageskarten und reduzierte Tickets (z. B. für Kinder, Jugendliche, Studenten, Gruppen etc.). Die ersten Züge fahren morgens in der Regel ab 05:30 Uhr, die letzten gegen Mitternacht.

S. 19

Famous London sights
1. A, **2.** C, **3.** D, **4.** B

Visiting London
1. British Museum, **2.** Oxford Street, **3.** Wembley Stadium, **4.** Tower Bridge

S. 20

Who will you see where?
1. B, **2.** A, **3.** C, **4.** D

The East End
1. C, **2.** B, **3.** F, **4.** H, **5.** A, **6.** G, **7.** D, **8.** E

S. 21

Cockney rhyming slang
1. D, **2.** B, **3.** C, **4.** A

Strange place names
1. D, **2.** C, **3.** A, **4.** B

Shop till you drop

S. 22

Well-known chains
1. D, **2.** A, **3.** C, **4.** B

A nation of shopkeepers
1. butcher, **2.** greengrocer, **3.** baker, **4.** hairdresser, **5.** florist

S. 23

Opening hours
1. B, **2.** C, **3.** D, **4.** A

Charity shops
1. C, **2.** D, **3.** E, **4.** A, **5.** F, **6.** B

S. 24

Asking for help
1. Could you tell me where the nearest pharmacy is?
2. I think I'd like to try a smaller size.
3. Can I return this if it doesn't fit?
4. At what time do you close today?

In the department store
1. D, **2.** A, **3.** B, **4.** C

Denken Sie daran, dass Konfektions- und Schuhgrößen in Großbritannien anders sind. Heutzutage steht zwar oft auch die europäische Größe auf dem Etikett, aber wer plant, in Großbritannien Klamotten zu kaufen (besonders wenn es ältere Kleidungsstücke aus einem **charity shop** sind!) wäre gut beraten, sich im Voraus schlau zu machen (z. B. im Internet).

Lösungen

1

S. 25

Buy British!
1. Twinings, **2.** Dr Martens, **3.** Rolls Royce, **4.** Vodafone

Companies
1. B, **2.** A, **3.** D, **4.** C

Westward Ho!

S. 28

Sights of the South West
1. C, **2.** B, **3.** D, **4.** A

Which county is it?
1. D, **2.** C, **3.** A, **4.** B, **5.** E

S. 29

Glastonbury fact file
1. C, **2.** D, **3.** C, **4.** C

Coastlines
Answer: B Devon

S. 30

Cornish pasties
1. flour, cold water; **2.** filling; **3.** beef; **4.** potatoes, onions

Preparation method
1. F, **2.** C, **3.** E, **4.** A, **5.** D, **6.** B

S. 31

Food and drink
1. clotted cream, **2.** Cheddar, **3.** cider, **4.** seafood

Fact or fiction?
False: 4, 6, 8

4. Das Surfen wurde zwar nicht in Newquay erfunden, aber die Stadt ist **„surf capital of the UK"**.
6. Die Fahrzeit von Land's End nach John O'Groats beträgt etwa 14 Stunden.
8. Löwen sind z. B. in den Zoos von Bristol und Newquay zu sehen, oder auch in dem bekannten Safaripark Longleat (Wiltshire).

Always look on the bright side

S. 32

Humour
1. E, **2.** A, **3.** B, **4.** C, **5.** D

S. 33

Find the jokers
1. E, **2.** F, **3.** A, **4.** H, **5.** B, **6.** C, **7.** D, **8.** G

Comedy films
1. A, **2.** D, **3.** C, **4.** B

S. 34

Jokes
1. B, **2.** A, **3.** G, **4.** D, **5.** F, **6.** H, **7.** E, **8.** C

Describing humour
1. dirty, **2.** black, **3.** ironic, **4.** witty, **5.** amusing, **6.** ridiculous

S. 35

Films and more
1. C, **2.** B, **3.** A, **4.** B

Restaurant jokes
1. D, **2.** C, **3.** A, **4.** B

It's grim up North – or is it?

S. 38

Cities of the North

1. Newcastle, B; **2.** Sheffield, A; **3.** Liverpool, C; **4.** Manchester, E; **5.** Leeds, D

The industrial past

1. C, **2.** D, **3.** A, **4.** B, **5.** E

S. 39

Actors and singers

1. C, **2.** D, **3.** B, **4.** A

Dame Judi Dench gilt als eine der erfolgreichsten britischen Schauspielerinnen aller Zeiten und ist für ihre Arbeit auf der Bühne, im Fernsehen und in Kinofilmen mehrfach ausgezeichnet worden, unter anderem auch von der Queen. Ihre bis dato sechs Oscar-Nominierungen erhielt sie, als sie bereits über 60 war. Sie war zudem die erste Frau, die die Figur „M" in den James Bond-Filmen gespielt hat.

Tourist attractions

1. C, **2.** D, **3.** A, **4.** B
Reihenfolge: 1. B, **2.** D, **3.** C, **4.** A

Hadrian's Wall wurde 122-128 von den Römern als Grenzbefestigungssystem erbaut. **York Minster**, Baubeginn circa 1220, wurde 1472 fertig gestellt. Der **Blackpool Tower** wurde 1894 eingeweiht, wobei ihm der Pariser Eiffelturm als Vorbild diente. 1998 wurde der Bau des **Angel of the North** abgeschlossen.

S. 40

Facts and figures

1. paint, above; **2.** medieval, big; **3.** border, hikers; **4.** wider, in

The North-South divide

1. D, **2.** E, **3.** A, **4.** B, **5.** C, **6.** F

S. 41

Food specialities

1. D, **2.** B, **3.** C, **4.** A

Northern brands

1. B, **2.** D, **3.** A, **4.** C

Meet the royals

S. 42

Historical periods

1. A, **2.** D, **3.** B, **4.** E, **5.** C

Politics and the monarchy

1. Stuart, **2.** Tudor, **3.** Edwardian, **4.** Regency, **5.** Victorian

S. 43

Official residences

4 Palace of Westminster

Der **Palace of Westminster** war bis 1529 königliche Residenz, aber heute ist er besser bekannt als **Houses of Parliament**, dem Sitz des britischen Parlaments. **Windsor Castle** befindet sich westlich von London, während **Balmoral** in Schottland liegt.

Royal sightseeing

1. B, **2.** B, **3.** C, **4.** A, **5.** B

S. 44

Royal ladies and gentlemen

1. king, **2.** princess, **3.** earl, **4.** duchess

The royal family

1. husband, **2.** adopted, **3.** brand, **4.** Eve, **5.** million euros, **6.** birthdays, **7.** to, **8.** than

Lösungen

S. 45

More royal names and titles

Across: 2. crown, **3.** Diana, **5.** Majesty, **7.** Highness, **9.** Commonwealth, **11.** George
Down: 1. Edward, **2.** Cambridge, **4.** Anne, **6.** Charles, **8.** Andrew, **10.** Henry

Scotland the Brave

S. 48

Scotland's economy

1. D, **2.** C, **3.** A, **4.** E, **5.** B

Cities in Scotland

1. B, **2.** E, **3.** D, **4.** A, **5.** C

S. 49

About Scotland

1. B, **2.** C, **3.** C, **4.** B, **5.** A

Tourist destinations

1. D, **2.** B, **3.** C, **4.** A

S. 50

Inventive Scots

1. C, **2.** D, **3.** E, **4.** A, **5.** B

Eine Art Regenmantel wurde 1824 von dem Glasgower Chemiker **Charles Macintosh** erfunden. Bis heute bezeichnet die Kurzform **mac** überall in Großbritannien einen leichten Regenmantel.

Scottish culture

1. Wallace, **2.** shortbread, **3.** haggis, **4.** Highlands, **5.** bagpipes, **6.** Nessie

S. 51

Scottish words

1. B, **2.** C, **3.** A, **4.** D, **5.** B

Scotland fact file

1. D, **2.** A, **3.** E, **4.** B, **5.** C

This sporting life

S. 52

British sport

1. G, **2.** H, **3.** A, **4.** C, **5.** D, **6.** E, **7.** F, **8.** B

Spricht man in Großbritannien von **football** (oder kurz **footy**), dann ist das weltweit bekannte Fußballspiel gemeint. Der Begriff **soccer**, hergeleitet von **association football**, wird in den USA, Australien, Neuseeland und Kanada bevorzugt, um einen klaren Unterschied zu anderen Formen des Fußballs (wie z. B. **American football**) zu machen.

History of sport

1. B, **2.** C, **3.** D, **4.** A

This Sporting Life (zu Deutsch *Lockender Lorbeer*) – so heißt ein berühmter Film des **British New Wave** aus dem Jahr 1963, in dem die Geschichte eines Rugby spielenden Bergarbeiters aus Yorkshire erzählt wird.

S. 53

Sport in films

1. D, **2.** E, **3.** A, **4.** B, **5.** C

Rules of the game

1. A, **2.** D, **3.** A and D, **4.** B, **5.** C, **6.** B, **7.** D, **8.** C

S. 54

Idioms from sport

1. D, **2.** E, **3.** A, **4.** C, **5.** F, **6.** B

Sport vocabulary

1. league, **2.** stadium, **3.** coach, **4.** result, **5.** pitch, **6.** trainers, **7.** court, **8.** goggles

S. 55

Disciplines
1. badminton, **2.** baseball, **3.** croquet, **4.** squash, **5.** pool, **6.** golf, **7.** boxing, **8.** darts

Wales – The Land of Song

S. 58

Wales
True: 1, 3, 5, 6, 9
False: 2, 4, 7, 8, 10

Welsh slate
1. E, **2.** C, **3.** A, **4.** F, **5.** D, **6.** G, **7.** B, **8.** H

Wer mehr über die walisische Schieferindustrie erfahren möchte, kann sich im **National Slate Museum** in Llanberis im Norden von Wales informieren. Noch abenteuerlicher geht es in den **Llechwedd Slate Caverns** zu (nahe Blaenau Ffestiniog, ebenfalls in Nordwales), wo man eine unterirdische Tour durch die Schieferhöhlen machen kann.

S. 59

Welsh celebrities
1. C, **2.** E, **3.** A, **4.** B, **5.** D

Sightseeing in Wales
1. C, **2.** A, **3.** B, **4.** D

S. 60

Facts about Wales
1. speciality, **2.** Library, **3.** speak, **4.** travel, **5.** seaside, **6.** ports, **7.** oldest, **8.** foreign

A Welsh snack
1. B, **2.** B, **3.** A, **4.** A, **5.** B

S. 61

Welsh and German
1. D, **2.** C, **3.** A, **4.** B
Übersetzungen:
A bell *(Glocke)*, B carrots *(Möhren)*, C window *(Fenster)*, D rabbit *(Kaninchen)*

Die walisische Sprache ist eine der ältesten lebendigen Sprachen Europas und gehört zu der keltischen Sprachenfamilie (wie auch z. B. Gälisch und Bretonisch). Manche der Ähnlichkeiten zwischen dem Walisischen und dem Deutschen gehen auf gemeinsame Einflüsse aus dem Lateinischen zurück.

Highest, longest, largest
1. Severn, **2.** Cardiff, **3.** Snowdon, **4.** St David's

On the roads and rails

S. 62

Road signs
1. C, **2.** B, **3.** C, **4.** D, **5.** C

S. 63

Vocabulary of driving
1. F, **2.** H, **3.** G, **4.** D, **5.** E, **6.** I, **7.** L, **8.** A, **9.** C, **10.** K, **11.** B, **12.** J

Rules of the road
1. C, **2.** D, **3.** A, **4.** B, **5.** E

Für die generellen Geschwindigkeitsbegrenzungen in Großbritannien gilt folgendes: in geschlossenen Ortschaften 30 mph (48 km/h); außerhalb geschlossener Ortschaften 40 mph (64 km/h); auf Landstraßen (**A roads**) 60 mph (96 km/h); auf Autobahnen (**motorways**) 70 mph (112 km/h).

Lösungen

1

LÖSUNGEN

S. 64

Using public transport
1. D, **2.** C, **3.** A, **4.** B, **5.** B, **6.** A

Saving money
1. cheaper, **2.** advance, **3.** discount,
4. single, **5.** children

S. 65

More public transport
1. coach, **2.** decker, **3.** cab, **4.** connection,
5. conductor, **6.** Express

Taxi!
1. D, **2.** A, **3.** B, **4.** E, **5.** C

Do you fancy a drink?

S. 68

Tea break
1. E, **2.** D, **3.** A, **4.** F, **5.** H, **6.** C, **7.** B, **8.** G

Afternoon tea
3 Filled baguette

Die zum **afternoon tea** servierten **sandwiches** sind in der Regel sehr delikat (z. B. mit Kresse oder Gurke als Füllung). Die Kuchenauswahl ist etwas flexibler, aber **Victoria sponge** und **scones** sind häufig dabei. Der aus Südwestengland bekannte **cream tea** besteht meistens aus **scones** mit **clotted cream** und **strawberry jam**.

S. 69

The tea ceremony
True: 1, 4
False: 2, 3, 5

Tea quiz
1. Earl Grey, **2.** Assam, **3.** herbal,
4. East India, **5.** breakfast , **6.** Scones

S. 70

Pub culture
1. C, **2.** D, **3.** B, **4.** B, **5.** D

Dass die Briten warmes Bier bevorzugen, stimmt nicht ganz. Geschmacksintensive Sorten, wie **stout** oder **bitter** werden traditionsgemäß bei Kellertemperatur (10–14°C) serviert, damit ihr subtiler Geschmack optimal zur Geltung kommt. **Lager**, nach kontinentaleuropäischem Vorbild gebraut, wird meistens gekühlt serviert.

Pub snacks
1. C, **2.** D, **3.** A, **4.** B
Not usually served in a pub: D pretzel

Pork scratchings kann etwa mit „(Schinken-)Speckchips" übersetzt werden; sie bestehen aus Schweineschwarte und sind daher nichts für Vegetarier. Kartoffelchips heißen übrigens überall in Großbritannien und Irland **crisps** – und nicht **chips**, denn das sind Pommes! – und sind in vielen verschiedenen Geschmacksrichtungen erhältlich.

S. 71

Beer types
1. C, **2.** B, **3.** A

Drinks with little or no alcohol
1. E, **2.** A, **3.** B, **4.** C, **5.** D

Small talk at the pub
1. D, **2.** E, **3.** A, **4.** C, **5.** B, **6.** F

Glorious grub

S. 72

British food brands
1. D, **2.** A, **3.** B, **4.** C

Eating internationally
1. Chinese, **2.** Indian, **3.** British, **4.** Italian, **5.** Thai

S. 73

Roast dinner
1. A, **2.** C, **3.** D, **4.** B

Traditional British dishes
1. C, **2.** A, **3.** D, **4.** B

Grub ist eine umgangssprachliche Bezeichnung für „Essen" oder auch „Fressalien". Man findet diesen Begriff etwa in Redewendungen wie **pub grub** (typisches Kneipenessen) oder **„Grub's up!"** („Essen fassen!").

S. 74

False friends
1. G, **2.** A, **3.** C, **4.** D

Manche Wörter im Bereich Essen und Trinken haben mehr als eine Bedeutung: z. B. **hot** bedeutet sowohl „heiß" als auch „scharf", während **pepper** sowohl „Pfeffer" als auch (manchmal im Plural) „Paprikagemüse" heißt.

Sandwich culture
1. chains, **2.** Wholemeal, **3.** Filled roll, **4.** toasted, **5.** Club

S. 75

English breakfast
black pudding, baked beans, tomatoes, mushrooms, scrambled eggs, bacon, toast, sausages, orange juice

Let's celebrate!

S. 78

The fifth of November
1. F, **2.** E, **3.** A, **4.** G, **5.** C, **6.** B, **7.** H, **8.** D

Celebrations
1. D, **2.** C, **3.** A, **4.** B

S. 79

Celebrating differently
1. B, **2.** A, **3.** C, **4.** A

Der britische und irische Muttertag (**Mother's Day** oder **Mothering Sunday**) wird immer am dritten Sonntag vor Ostern gefeiert. Früher besuchten Gläubige an diesem Tag ihre Mutterkirche, wodurch die Assoziation mit Müttern entstand.

Traditions and superstitions
1. C, **2.** E, **3.** D, **4.** B, **5.** A

S. 80

Party small talk
1. C, **2.** B, **3.** C, **4.** A

Reasons to celebrate
1. D, **2.** E, **3.** A, **4.** C, **5.** B

S. 81

Celebration customs
Yes: 1, 2, 3, 7
No: 4, 5, 6, 8

7.30 pm for 8 heißt meistens, dass man ab 19:30 Uhr jederzeit willkommen ist und gegen 20 Uhr das Essen serviert wird. Auf Festen wartet man meistens, bis man miteinander ins Gespräch kommt, bevor man sich namentlich vorstellt. Beim Ankommen genügen meist ein freundliches Lächeln und ein allgemeiner Gruß in die Runde.

Wedding traditions
3 (Polterabend)

Lösungen

Einen Polterabend gibt es im Vorfeld britischer Hochzeiten nicht. Üblich ist eine Art Junggesellenabschied, der meistens ein paar Wochen vor der Hochzeit stattfindet: eine **stag night** für den Bräutigam und seine Freunde sowie eine **hen night** für die Braut und ihre Freundinnen.

Politics and news media

S. 82

British politics
1. C, **2.** A, **3.** A, **4.** B

Elections and parliament
1. D, **2.** E, **3.** F, **4.** B, **5.** A, **6.** C, **7.** H, **8.** G

Wahlen im Vereinigten Königreich finden stets donnerstags statt. Warum das so ist, weiß man nicht genau, aber eine beliebte Theorie besagt, dass Arbeiter früher immer freitags ihren Lohn bekamen. Donnerstags hatten sie meist kein Geld mehr für Bier und waren so nüchtern genug, um wählen zu gehen.

S. 83

Prime ministers
1. Winston Churchill, **2.** Margaret Thatcher, **3.** Tony Blair

More about British politics
1. C, **2.** B, **3.** E, **4.** A, **5.** D

S. 84

Newspaper culture
1. broadsheet: C, F, G, J
2. tabloid: A, B, D, E, H, I

Zu beachten ist, dass das Wort **news** nur im Singular verwendet wird (**The news is good.**).

Other news media
1. sites, **2.** breaking, **3.** blogs, **4.** newsreader, **5.** politicians, **6.** broadcast

S. 85

News and politics
1. B, **2.** C, **3.** B

British newspapers
1. *Mirror* (T), **2.** *Times* (B), **3.** *Guardian* (B), **4.** *Sun* (T), **5.** *Telegraph* (B), **6.** *Daily Mail* (T)

Shakespeare's country

S. 88

Birmingham
1. E, **2.** C, **3.** F, **4.** B, **5.** G, **6.** A, **7.** D, **8.** H

Other towns and cities
1. D, **2.** C, **3.** A, **4.** B

S. 89

The Midlands
1. B, **2.** B, **3.** C, **4.** C

Ob man das Schokoerlebnis der **Cadbury World** erleben oder doch lieber das größte Motorradmuseum der Welt im **National Motorcycle Museum** besichtigen möchte – hier sind auf alle Fälle spannende Ausflüge geboten.

The industrial past and present
1. C, **2.** D, **3.** E, **4.** A, **5.** B

Für das Land Mordor in ***Lord of the Rings*** wurde der Autor **J. R. R. Tolkien** wahrscheinlich vom **Black Country** inspiriert, denn in der mittelirdischen Sprache Sindarin bedeutet der Name „schwarzes Land". Tolkien selbst wuchs in der Nähe von Birmingham auf.

S. 90

Robin Hood
1. A, **2.** B, **3.** C, **4.** A, **5.** C

Midlands specialities
1. D, **2.** C, **3.** A, **4.** B

S. 91

Shakespeare's life and works
False: 3, 8, 10

Shakespeare nannte seinen Sohn **Hamnet**. Shakespeares Vater selbst konnte vermutlich weder schreiben noch lesen und auch William selbst verließ bereits mit 15 die Schule. Zwischen 1585 und 1592 zog Shakespeare dann nach London. Dort gibt es heute das **Shakespeare's Globe**, einen Nachbau des elisabethanischen Theaters, an dem Shakespeare selbst tätig war.

Shakespeare quotations
1. C, **2.** A, **3.** E, **4.** B, **5.** D

On screen: TV and film

S. 92

British TV and film
1. E, **2.** A, **3.** F, **4.** B, **5.** D, **6.** C

History of the BBC
1. G, **2.** C, **3.** E, **4.** D, **5.** A, **6.** H, **7.** B, **8.** F

S. 93

Murder mysteries and thrillers
1. E, **2.** D, **3.** B, **4.** C, **5.** A

British films
1. D, **2.** E, **3.** C, **4.** B, **5.** A

S. 94

Film and TV vocabulary
1. C, **2.** A, **3.** A, **4.** C, **5.** A, **6.** B

Different genres
1. action, **2.** adventure, **3.** tragedy, **4.** thriller, **5.** fantasy

S. 95

Bond, James Bond
1. *Russia*, **2.** *Diamonds*, **3.** *Tomorrow*, **4.** *Casino*

British Oscar winners
1. G, **2.** E, **3.** A, **4.** D, **5.** F, **6.** C, **7.** H, **8.** B

Der bisher erfolgreichste britische Film bei den amerikanischen Oscar-Verleihungen war ***The English Patient***, der 1996 neun **Academy Awards** gewann. Die Filme ***Gandhi*** und ***Slumdog Millionaire*** gewannen 1981 bzw. 2009 jeweils acht Oscare.

The Emerald Isle

S. 98

Ireland's main cities
1. B, **2.** D, **3.** C, **4.** A, **5.** E

The economy of Ireland
1. G, **2.** C, **3.** A, **4.** H, **5.** D, **6.** F, **7.** B, **8.** E

S. 99

The Republic of Ireland
1. C, **2.** D, **3.** B, **4.** A, **5.** E

Die Farben und Zusammensetzung der irischen Flagge haben symbolische Bedeutung: Grün soll für die Insel und die katholische Bevölkerung stehen, Orange für die protestantische Bevölkerung, während das Weiß den Frieden zwischen den beiden Konfessionen repräsentieren soll.

The road to peace
1. D, **2.** B, **3.** F, **4.** A, **5.** E, **6.** C

Lösungen

S. 100

Places to visit

1. C, **2.** B, **3.** D, **4.** A

Famous Irish artists

1. E, **2.** C, **3.** B, **4.** A, **5.** D

S. 101

Irish English

1. C, **2.** C, **3.** B, **4.** A, **5.** A

Guinness

1. brewery, **2.** countries, **3.** attractions, **4.** glasses, **5.** Patrick, **6.** seconds

Music and art in Britain

S. 102

British bands

1. Led Zeppelin, **2.** The Police, **3.** The Smiths, **4.** Oasis, **5.** Coldplay

Music & Co

1. B, **2.** C, **3.** D, **4.** A

S. 103

Andrew Lloyd Webber

1. C, **2.** D, **3.** B, **4.** A

British composers

1. C, **2.** A, **3.** D, **4.** B

S. 104

Tate Modern

1. F, **2.** D, **3.** H, **4.** A, **5.** C, **6.** B, **7.** E, **8.** G

British artists

1. D, **2.** A, **3.** B, **4.** C

Britart wurde 1992 als Begriff geprägt. Der Name deutet auf eine Gruppe damals junger Künstler hin (auch als **Young British Artists** bekannt), die vorwiegend im Bereich der Konzeptkunst tätig waren. **Tracy Emin**, **Damien Hirst** und **Sarah Lucas** sind wohl die bekanntesten Vertreter dieser Bewegung.

S. 105

Music and art

Across: 2. queen, **4.** Albert, **8.** Proms, **9.** Hirst
Down: 1. Adele, **3.** Banksy, **5.** Beatles, **6.** Rattle, **7.** Freud

A

A road	*Landstraße*
above	*über, oberhalb*
according to	*laut*
actor	*Schauspieler*
actress	*Schauspielerin*
actual(ly)	*eigentlich*
to **adapt**	*adaptieren; umschreiben*
address	*Ansprache*
to **address sb**	*jdn. ansprechen*
to **adopt**	*adoptieren; annehmen*
adventure	*Abenteuer*
aeroplane	*Flugzeug*
to **affect**	*eine Auswirkung ausüben, beeinflussen*
afraid	*Angst haben*
afternoon tea	*Tee mit Scones und Streichrahm*
age	*(Zeit-)Alter*
to **agree**	*sich einigen; zustimmen*
agreement	*Vertrag, Abkommen, Vereinbarung*
agriculture	*Landwirtschaft*
aim	*Ziel*
airport	*Flughafen*
ale	*Ale (Bier)*
All Saints' Day	*Allerheiligen*
alive	*lebend; lebendig*
alliance	*Bündnis*
to **allow**	*erlauben*
ambulance	*Krankenwagen*
amusing	*amüsant*
ancestry	*Abstammung*
ancient	*uralt*
angel	*Engel*
annual	*jährlich*
apart from	*außer*
to **appear**	*erscheinen*
appearance	*Erscheinen, Auftritt*
to **approve**	*genehmigen*
Arrivals	*Ankunftsbereich (z. B. Flughafen)*
art	*Kunst*
artist	*Künstler, Künstlerin*
to **ask**	*bitten, fragen*
to **attract**	*anziehen*
audience	*Publikum*
author	*Autor(in)*
average	*durchschnittlich*
award	*Preis, Auszeichnung*

B

backwards	*rückwärts*
bacon	*(Schinken-)Speck*
bagpipes	*Dudelsack*
baked beans	*(weiße) Bohnen in Tomatensoße*
baker	*Bäcker(in)*
baking powder	*Backpulver*
bank holiday	*gesetzlicher Feiertag*
to **baptize sb**	*jdn. taufen*
bargain	*Schnäppchen*
based on	*basierend auf*
bat	*Schlagholz, Schläger*
batsman	*Schlagmann*
batter	*Backteig*
beach	*Strand*
bean	*Bohne*
to **become**	*werden*
beef	*Rindfleisch*
beholder	*Betrachter(in)*
to **believe**	*glauben*
bell	*Glocke*
to **belong to sth**	*etw. angehören, zu etw. gehören*
below	*unter(halb)*
belt	*Gürtel*
to **bend**	*krümmen*
Best wishes	*Mit freundlichen Grüßen*
biscuit	*Keks*
bitter	*Bitter (dunkles Bier)*
black	*schwarz*
black pudding	*Blutwurst*
blackboard	*Tafel (z. B. im Klassenzimmer)*
blend	*Mischung*
blended	*zusammengemischt*
to **blow up**	*explodieren, in die Luft sprengen*
boiled	*gekocht (z. B. Gemüse)*
boiling	*kochend*
bonfire	*Scheiterhaufen; Freudenfeuer*
boot	*Stiefel*
border	*Grenze*
to **borrow**	*sich ausleihen*
Boxing Day	*zweiter Weihnachtsfeiertag*
boxing match	*Boxwettkampf*
bowler	*(Ball-)Werfer(in)*
brand	*Marke*
brave	*mutig*
break	*Pause*
breakdown	*Autopanne*
breakfast	*Frühstück*
breathtaking	*atemberaubend*
breaking news	*Eilmeldung*
to **brew**	*ziehen lassen (z. B. Tee); brauen (z. B. Bier)*
brewery	*Brauerei*
brick	*Backstein*
bridge	*Brücke*
bright	*hell, leuchtend; heiter*
British Isles	*Britische Inseln*
to **broadcast**	*senden, übertragen*
broadcasting station	*Fernsehsender, Radiosender*
broadsheet	*großformatige, seriöse Zeitung*

Wortverzeichnis

broken	*kaputt*
to **brush**	*bürsten; anpinseln*
bubble and squeak	*Essen aus (Grün-)Kohl, Kartoffeln und ggf. Fleisch*
to **build**	*(er)bauen*
building	*Gebäude*
burned	*verbrannt*
to **bury**	*begraben*
busy	*belebt; beschäftigt*
butcher	*Metzger(in)*
butterfly	*Schmetterling*
by yourself	*allein*

C

cab	*Taxi*
cabbage	*Kohl, Kraut*
cabby	*Taxifahrer(in) (ugs.)*
cake	*Kuchen*
to **call**	*nennen; (an)rufen*
to **campaign for sth**	*für etw. eintreten*
canal	*Schifffahrtskanal*
capital	*Hauptstadt*
careful	*vorsichtig*
castle	*Burg*
cat	*Katze*
to **celebrate**	*feiern*
celebration	*Fest, Feier*
celebrity	*Prominente(r)*
cellar	*Keller*
Celt	*Kelte, Keltin*
century	*Jahrhundert*
chain	*Kette*
channel	*(Fernseh-)Kanal*
chariot	*(Streit-)Wagen*
charity shop	*gemeinnütziger Gebrauchtwarenladen*
charity work	*Engagement für wohltätige Zwecke; ehrenamtliche Arbeit*
chat	*kurzes Gespräch, Unterhaltung*
cheap	*billig, preiswert*
cheers	*Prost*
chicken	*Hähnchen; Huhn*
chieftain	*Oberhaupt*
chimney	*Schornstein*
chips	*Pommes (frites)*
city	*(Groß-)Stadt*
to **chop**	*hacken; schneiden*
christening	*Taufe*
Christmas	*Weihnachten*
Christmas Day	*erster Weihnachtsfeiertag*
Christmas Eve	*Heiligabend*
church	*Kirche*
cider	*Apfelwein*
circle	*Kreis*
clay	*Knet, Lehm*
clean	*sauber*
cliff	*Klippe*
clone	*Klon*
to **close**	*schließen*
closing ceremony	*(Ab-)Schlussfeier*
clotted cream	*Streichrahm*
coach	*Trainer(in); Reisebus; Waggon*
coal	*Kohle*
coast	*Küste*
comedian	*Komiker(in)*
companion	*Begleiter(in)*
company	*Firma, Unternehmen*
competition	*Wettbewerb*
composer	*Komponist(in)*
conductor	*Dirigent(in); Schaffner(in)*
congratulation	*Glückwunsch, Gratulation*
to **connect**	*verbinden*
connection	*Verbindung*
to **conquer**	*erobern*
conqueror	*Eroberer, Eroberin*
to **consider**	*betrachten*
to **consist of**	*bestehen aus*
to **console**	*(hinweg)trösten*
contagious	*ansteckend*
to **contain**	*enthalten, beinhalten*
contemporary	*zeitgenössisch*
cordial	*Sirup*
corner	*Ecke*
cotton	*Baumwolle*
to **count**	*(aus)zählen*
countess	*Gräfin*
countless	*unzählig*
county	*Grafschaft*
course	*Kurs; Lauf*
cover	*Hülle; Abdeckung*
to **cover**	*bedecken; überziehen*
crab	*Krebs(fleisch)*
crackling	*(Braten-)Kruste*
cream tea	*Tee mit Scones und Streichrahm*
crisps	*Chips*
croquet	*Krocket(spiel)*
to **cross**	*überqueren*
crossword	*Kreuzworträtsel*
cruel	*gemein; grausam*
cup	*Tasse*
cupboard	*Schrank*
currant	*Korinthe*
currency	*Währung*
custom	*Gewohnheit, Tradition*
customs	*Zoll*
cycling	*(Fahr-)Radfahren*
cyclist	*(Fahr-)Radfahrer(in)*

D

dangerous	*gefährlich*
dark	*dunkel*
date	*Verabredung; Rendevous*

date of birth	*Geburtsdatum*
day ticket	*Tages(fahr)karte*
dead	*tot*
delayed	*verspätet*
delicate	*zerbrechlich*
department store	*Kaufhaus*
to **describe**	*beschreiben*
desperate	*verzweifelt*
destination	*(Reise-)Ziel*
diary	*Kalender; Tagebuch*
different	*anders, unterschiedlich*
dirty	*schmutzig*
disappointment	*Enttäuschung*
disaster	*Katastrophe; Unglück*
discontent	*Unzufriedenheit*
discount	*Rabatt, Ermäßigung*
to **discover**	*entdecken*
dish	*Gericht (Essen)*
display	*Feuerwerk; Ausstellung, Vorführung*
to **display**	*zeigen, zur Schau stellen*
distillery	*Destillerie*
diversion	*Umleitung*
divide	*Kluft; Trennlinie*
doctor's surgery	*Arztpraxis*
documentary	*Dokumentarfilm*
dog	*Hund*
to **donate**	*spenden*
double-decker	*Doppeldecker*
down-to-earth	*bodenständig*
dragon	*Drache*
to **dress**	*sich kleiden; sich anziehen*
dress	*Kleid*
driving licence	*Führerschein*
to **drop**	*(um)fallen*
dual carriageway	*zweispurige Fahrbahn*
duchess	*Herzogin*
duke	*Herzog*
during	*während*
dustbin	*Mülleimer*

E

earl	*Graf*
to **earn**	*verdienen*
Easter	*Ostern*
eastern	*östlich, Ost-*
economy	*Wirtschaft*
egg yolk	*Eigelb*
eldest	*älteste(r, s)*
to **elect**	*wählen*
election	*Wahl*
the **Emerald Isle**	*die Grüne Insel (Irland)*
empire	*Reich*
employee	*Arbeitnehmer(in)*
employer	*Arbeitgeber(in)*
empress	*Kaiserin*
to **endeavour**	*bestreben*
enemy	*Feind(in)*
engagement	*Verlobung*
engineer	*Ingenieur(in)*
enigma	*Rätsel*
to **enjoy**	*genießen; gefallen*
essential	*(unbedingt) erforderlich*
estate	*Anwesen*
event	*Ereignis, Anlass*
evidence	*Beweis*
exhibition	*Ausstellung*
expensive	*teuer*
to **experience**	*erleben, erfahren*
explosive	*Sprengstoff*

F

fabric	*Stoff (Textilien)*
face	*Gesicht*
factory	*Fabrik*
fair	*schön*
to **fancy sth**	*etw. wollen, etw. mögen*
famous	*berühmt*
fare	*Fahrpreis*
fashion designer	*Modedesigner(in)*
fashionable	*modisch*
favourite	*Lieblings-*
fear	*Angst*
feature	*Bestandteil; Kennzeichen*
ferry	*Fähre*
to **fetch**	*holen*
to **fight**	*kämpfen, sich streiten*
file	*Ordner; Akte; Datei*
filled	*gefüllt, belegt (z. B. Brötchen)*
filling	*Füllung*
film director	*Regisseur(in)*
fine(ly)	*fein*
to **finish**	*(be)enden, aufhören*
fire brigade	*Feuerwehr*
to **fit**	*passen (z. B. Kleidung)*
floor	*(Fuß-)Boden*
florist	*Florist(in)*
flour	*Mehl*
flower	*Blume*
fly	*Fliege*
to **focus on sth**	*sich auf etw. konzentrieren*
fog	*Nebel*
to **fold**	*falten*
fool	*Narr, Närrin*
foolish	*töricht*
footwear	*Schuhe, Schuhwerk*
for ever	*bis in alle Ewigkeit, immer und ewig*
foreign	*ausländisch*
foreign secretary	*Außenminister(in)*
former	*ehemalig*
to **found**	*gründen*
founder	*Gründer(in)*
fox	*Fuchs*
fridge	*Kühlschrank*

Wortverzeichnis

	fried	*(an)gebraten*
	frog	*Frosch*
	frog's legs	*Froschschenkel*
	fruit	*Obst, Frucht*
	fuel	*Treibstoff*
	full monty	*das volle Programm (ugs.)*
	fun	*Spaß*
	funeral	*Beerdigung*
	funny	*lustig, komisch*

G

	Gaelic	*Gälisch*
	garlic	*Knoblauch*
to	**get lost**	*sich verirren*
	giant	*Riese, Riesin*
	giant	*riesig sein*
	gift	*Geschenk*
	glen	*Tal*
	gloves	*Handschuhe*
to	**go out with sb**	*sich mit jdm. verabreden; mit jdm. ausgehen*
	goal	*Tor (z. B. Fußball)*
	goggles	*Taucherbrille*
	golf course	*Golfplatz*
	Good Friday	*Karfreitag*
	gorge	*Schlucht*
	gossip	*Klatsch, Tratsch*
to	**govern**	*regieren*
	government	*Regierung*
to	**grate**	*reiben (z. B. Käse)*
	gravestone	*Grabstein*
	greengrocer	*Obst- und Gemüsehändler(in)*
	greenhouse	*Gewächshaus*
	grim	*kalt und grau, unwirtlich*
to	**grow**	*wachsen; angebaut werden*
	grub	*Essen, Fressalien (ugs.)*
	Grub's up!	*Essen fassen! (ugs.)*
	gutter press	*Skandalpresse*

H

	haberdashery	*Kurzwaren*
	haddock	*Schellfisch*
	Hadrian's Wall	*Hadrianswall*
	haggis	*schottisches Gericht: gekochter Schafsmagen gefüllt mit Innereien und Haferschrot*
	hail	*Hagel*
	haircut	*Haarschnitt; Frisur*
	hairdresser	*Friseur(in)*
	hall	*Halle*
	handicrafts	*Handarbeit; Bastelarbeit*
	hardly	*kaum*
	harp	*Harfe*
	haven	*Zufluchtsort*
	head	*Kopf; Oberhaupt*
	head of state	*Staatsoberhaupt*
	headline	*Schlagzeile*
	health secretary	*Gesundheitsminister(in)*
	healthy	*gesund*
	heart	*Herz(stück)*
	heavy	*schwer*
	height	*Höhe*
	hen night	*Jungesellinnen-abschiedsparty*
	herbal tea	*Kräutertee*
	herbs	*Kräuter*
	heritage	*Erbe*
	hero	*Held*
to	**hide**	*(sich) verstecken*
	high	*hoch*
	high street	*Haupteinkaufsstraße*
	Highway Code	*Straßenverkehrsordnung*
	hiker	*Wanderer(in)*
to	**hire**	*mieten*
	history	*Geschichte*
to	**hit**	*schlagen*
	hitchhiker	*Anhalter(in), Tramper(in)*
	hole	*Loch*
the	**Holy Grail**	*der Heilige Gral*
	home secretary	*Innenminister(in)*
	honest	*ehrlich*
	horse	*Pferd*
	horseradish	*Meerrettich*
	hosiery	*Strumpfwaren*
	hot	*heiß; scharf*
	hound	*Jagdhund*
the	**House of Commons**	*das britische Unterhaus*
the	**House of Lords**	*das britische Oberhaus*
to	**house**	*beherbergen*
	housewarming party	*Einweihungsparty*
	huge	*riesig*
	human	*menschlich*
	husband	*Ehemann*

I

	idiom	*(idiomatische) Redewendung*
	immediately	*sofort, gleich*
	important	*wichtig*
	impressive	*beeindruckend, imposant*
to	**imprison**	*einsperren*
	in advance	*im Voraus*
to	**include**	*beinhalten*
	in-depth	*vertieft, gründlich*
	influential	*einflussreich*
	ingredient	*Zutat*
	insurance	*Versicherung*
to	**introduce yourself**	*sich vorstellen*
to	**invade**	*einmarschieren*
to	**invent**	*erfinden*
	inventive	*erfinderisch*
to	**investigate**	*ermitteln, nachforschen*
	investment	*Investition*

invitation	*Einladung*
the **Iron Lady**	*die eiserne Lady*
irresistible	*unwiderstehlich*
island	*Insel*
isle	*Eiland, (kleine) Insel*
item	*Gegenstand*

J

jewellery	*Schmuck*
to **join sb**	*sich zu jdm. gesellen*
joke	*Witz, Scherz*
journey	*Reise, Fahrt*

K

kettle	*Wasserkocher*
kilt	*Schottenrock*
kind	*Sorte, Art*
Kind regards	*Mit freundlichen Grüßen*
knife	*Messer*
knitwear	*Strickwaren*
to **know**	*kennen; wissen*
known	*bekannt*

L

Labour Day	*Tag der Arbeit*
lager	*Lagerbier (helles Bier)*
lamb	*Lamm(fleisch)*
landscape	*Landschaft*
lane	*(Fahr-)Spur*
language	*Sprache*
late	*(zu) spät*
laughter	*Lachen, Gelächter*
laverbread	*walisische Spezialität aus Seetang*
law	*Gesetz, Rechtsystem*
to **lead**	*leiten, führen*
league	*Liga*
leg	*Bein*
leisure	*Freizeit*
lentil	*Linse (Hülsenfrucht)*
leprechaun	*Kobold*
letter	*Brief, Buchstabe*
library	*Bibliothek*
licence fee	*Rundfunk- und Fernsehgebühren, Lizenzgebühr*
light	*hell; leicht*
to **light (up)**	*anzünden; aufleuchten*
lightning	*Blitz*
limit	*Begrenzung*
lingerie	*Dessous; (Damen-)Unterwäsche*
link	*Verbindung; Link*
lion	*Löwe*
lively	*lebendig*
local	*örtlich, lokal*
to be **located**	*gelegen sein, liegen*
location	*Ortschaft*
loch	*See; Meeresarm*
to **look after sb / sth**	*sich um jmd. / etw. kümmern*
looking-glass	*Spiegel*
loose	*lose*
lord	*Herr*
to **lose**	*verlieren*
loud	*laut*
luck	*Glück*

M

mac	*Regenmantel*
mad	*verrückt*
magazine	*Zeitschrift*
mainly	*hauptsächlich*
malt	*Malz*
to **manufacture**	*herstellen, produzieren*
manufacturer	*Hersteller, Produzent*
manuscript	*Handschrift; Manuskript*
map	*Landkarte*
marina	*Yachthafen*
mark	*Fleck; Zeichen*
marmalade	*Orangenmarmelade*
married	*verheiratet*
match point	*Matchball (Tennis)*
mathematician	*Mathematiker(in)*
mayor	*Bürgermeister(in)*
maze	*Irrgarten, Labyrinth*
to **measure**	*(ab)messen*
media	*Medien*
medieval	*mittelalterlich*
to **meet**	*begegnen; treffen; sich kennenlernen*
to **melt**	*schmelzen*
member	*Mitglied*
memory	*Erinnerung*
merely	*lediglich*
meter	*Taxameter*
mice (pl.)	*Mäuse*
Middle England	*die (konservative) englische Mittelschicht*
middle-aged	*mittleren Alters*
to **mind sth**	*etw. ausmachen; etw. einzuwenden haben*
mining	*Bergbau*
minority	*Minderheit*
minster	*Münster*
mistake	*Fehler*
mistletoe	*Mistel(zweig)*
to **mix**	*(ver)mischen*
mixture	*Mischung*
monastery	*Kloster*
mother-in-law	*Schwiegermutter*
Mother's Day	*Muttertag*
motorcycle	*Motorrad*
motorway	*Autobahn*
mug	*Becher*
murder mystery	*Krimi*

mushroom	*Pilz*
mustard	*Senf*

N

national anthem	*Nationalhymne*
neck	*Hals*
New Year's Day	*Neujahr(stag)*
news	*Nachricht(en)*
news agency	*Nachrichtenagentur*
news conference	*Pressekonferenz*
newsagent's (shop)	*Zeitschriftengeschäft*
newsflash	*Kurzmeldung*
newsreader	*Nachrichtensprecher(in)*
nickname	*Spitzname*
nightdress	*Nachthemd*
noise	*Geräusch*
Norman	*Normanne, Normannin*
nurse	*Krankenpfleger(in)*

O

oak (tree)	*Eiche(nbaum)*
oats	*Hafer*
obsessed	*besessen*
office	*Büro*
offside	*abseits*
onion	*Zwiebel*
opening ceremony	*Eröffnungsfeier*
opening hours	*Öffnungszeiten*
opera singer	*Opernsänger(in)*
to **operate**	*betreiben, leiten*
to **order**	*bestellen*
originally	*ursprünglich*
to be **out of luck**	*kein Glück haben*
to be **out of the office**	*nicht im Büro sein*
to be **out of time**	*aus dem Takt sein*
outlandish	*sonderbar*
outside	*draußen*
to **own**	*besitzen*

P

paint	*(Anstrich-)Farbe, Lack*
painter	*Maler(in)*
palace	*Palast*
Pancake Day	*Faschingsdienstag*
paprika	*Paprika(gewürz)*
parking meter	*Parkuhr*
to **pass**	*vorbeigehen; vorbeifahren; überqueren*
passenger	*Passagier(in), Insasse, Inassin*
passport	*Reisepass*
pasty	*Pastete*
pastries	*Backwaren*
pastry	*Teig*
path	*(Fuß-)Weg*
pea	*Erbse*
peace	*Frieden*
peanut	*Erdnuss*
pedestrian	*Fußgänger(in)*
pen	*Stift*
penalty	*Strafpunkt; Elfmeter*
pencil	*Bleistift*
pepper	*Pfeffer; Paprikagemüse*
period	*Zeitalter, Epoche*
pharmacy	*Apotheke*
physicist	*Physiker(in)*
pie	*Pastete; Kuchen*
pineapple	*Ananas*
pitch	*Spielfeld*
place	*Ort*
plane	*Flugzeug*
play	*Theaterstück*
plot	*Komplott*
ploughman's lunch	*Mittagessen, das aus Brot, Käse, einer Art Chutney und Salat besteht*
pneumatic tyre	*Luftreifen*
poet	*Dichter(in)*
point	*Punkt*
polite	*höflich*
politician	*Politiker(in)*
politics	*Politik*
pool	*Poolbilliard*
poor	*arm*
popular	*beliebt; weit verbreitet*
pork	*Schweinefleisch*
pork scratchings	*(Schinken-)Speckchips*
port	*Hafen*
post office	*Postamt*
potato	*Kartoffel*
pottery	*Töpferei; Keramik*
to **pour**	*gießen; einschenken*
power station	*Kraftwerk*
powerful	*mächtig*
to **prepare**	*vor-, zubereiten*
present	*Geschenk*
prime minister	*Premierminister(in)*
prince	*Prinz*
princess	*Prinzessin*
probably	*wahrscheinlich*
programme	*Sendung*
to **proof**	*Beweis*
to **protect**	*schützen*
to **provide**	*liefern*
psychoanalyst	*Psychoanalytiker(in)*
pub grup	*typisches Kneipenessen (ugs.)*
public	*Öffentlichkeit*
public	*öffentlich*
public holiday	*gesetzlicher Feiertag*
public speaker	*öffentliche(r) Redner(in)*
public transport	*öffentlicher Verkehr; öffentliche Verkehrsmittel*
to **pull**	*ziehen*
to **pull a funny face**	*ein komisches Gesicht ziehen*

punchline	*Pointe*
to **push**	*drücken, schieben*

Q

quarry	*Steinbruch*
question	*Frage*
quotation	*Zitat*

R

rabbit	*Kaninchen*
racquet	*Tennisschläger*
rail	*Schiene, Bahn*
railway	*Eisenbahn*
rain	*Regen*
raincoat	*Regenjacke, -mantel*
to **raise money**	*Geld sammeln*
raisin	*Rosine*
raw	*roh*
raw material	*Rohstoff*
real ale	*Real Ale (nach traditioneller Art gebrautes Bier)*
reason	*Grund*
reasonable	*vernünftig*
recipe	*Rezept (Essen)*
to **recommend**	*empfehlen*
record label	*Plattenfirma*
regards	*Grüße*
register	*Register*
to **remember**	*sich erinnern; sich merken*
to **remind sb**	*jdn. erinnern*
to **replace**	*ersetzen*
to **reply**	*antworten*
to **re-roof**	*neu überdachen*
resident	*Einwohner(in)*
resort	*Urlaubsort*
result	*Ergebnis*
retail	*Verkauf*
to **retire**	*in Rente gehen*
to **return**	*zurückbringen*
return ticket	*Rückfahrkarte*
review	*Rezension, Kritik*
to **rhyme**	*sich reimen*
rich	*reich*
ridiculous	*lächerlich*
rights	*Rechte*
river	*Fluß*
road	*Straße*
roadworks	*Straßenarbeiten*
roast	*gebraten, Brat-*
roast dinner	*(Sonntags-)Braten*
robbery	*Raubüberfall*
rock	*Fels; Stein*
role	*Rolle (z. B. Theater)*
roll	*Brötchen*
Roman	*Römer(in)*
roof	*Dach*
roundabout	*Kreisverkehr*
to **row**	*rudern*
rubber	*Gummi*
rule	*Regel(ung)*
rural	*ländlich*

S

safety belt	*Sicherheitsgurt*
salt	*Salz*
saucepan	*Kochtopf*
saucer	*Untertasse*
sausage	*Wurst, Würstchen*
to **save**	*sparen*
sceptred	*hoheitlich*
schoolboy	*Schüler*
scientist	*(Natur-)Wissenschaftler(in)*
to **score**	*punkten, Punkte erzielen*
scrambled eggs	*Rühreier*
screen	*Kinoleinwand; Bildschirm; Blende; Sichtschirm; Schutz*
seafood	*Meeresfrüchte*
to **seal**	*versiegeln*
seaside	*See-, am Meer*
to **season**	*würzen, abschmecken*
season ticket	*Saisonkarte; Zeitkarte*
seat	*Sitz(platz)*
seaweed	*Seetang*
to **sell**	*verkaufen*
selling space	*Verkaufsfläche*
to **send**	*(ver)schicken*
sender	*Absender(in)*
to **separate**	*(sich) trennen*
to **serve**	*dienen; servieren*
service industry	*Dienstleistungsbranche*
to **set up**	*einrichten; aufbauen*
several	*mehrere*
to **sew**	*nähen*
shandy	*Radler, Alsterwasser*
shape	*Form*
share	*Anteil; Aktie*
to **share**	*teilen*
shave	*Rasur*
shed	*Schuppen*
sheep	*Schaf(e)*
shining	*glänzend, strahlend*
ship	*Schiff*
shipwreck	*Schiffbruch*
shopkeeper	*Ladeninhaber(in)*
shortbread	*Shortbread (Buttergebäck)*
to **show**	*zeigen*
shower	*Dusche; Regenschauer*
Shrove Tuesday	*Faschingsdienstag*
shuttle	*Transferservice (z. B. Flughafen)*
sick	*krank*
side dish	*Beilage*
sight	*Sehenswürdigkeit*
sightseeing	*Besichtigungen*

Wortverzeichnis

	sign	*Schild; Zeichen*
a	**sign of the times**	*ein Zeichen der Zeit*
to	**sign**	*unterschreiben*
	significance	*Bedeutung*
	silly	*albern; dumm*
	similar	*ähnlich*
	simply	*einfach(erweise)*
	single malt	*ungemischter Whisky*
	single ticket	*einfache Fahrt*
	site	*Seite (Internet)*
	size	*Größe*
	sketch	*Skizze*
	skirt	*Rock*
	slate	*Schiefer*
	slice	*Scheibe (z. B. Brot)*
to	**smoke**	*rauchen*
	smoked	*geraucht*
	smooth	*glatt; weich*
	snail	*Schnecke*
	snatch	*schneller Griff; Diebstahl*
	sock	*Socke*
	soft drink	*alkoholfreies Getränk*
	sole	*Sohle*
	soccer	*Fußball*
	soot	*Ruß*
	soup	*Suppe*
	spa	*Badeort, Heilbad*
	space	*Raum, Platz; Fläche; Weltraum*
	specialisation	*Spezialisierung*
	speciality	*Spezialität*
	speech	*Rede*
	speed	*Geschwindigkeit*
	speed limit	*Tempolimit*
	spicy	*würzig, scharf*
	spirits	*Spirituosen*
	sponge (cake)	*Biskuit(kuchen), Rührkuchen*
	spritzer	*Schorle*
	square mile	*Quadratmeile*
	squash	*Fruchtsaftkonzentrat*
	squeak	*Quietschen, Quieken*
	stadium	*Stadion*
	stag night	*Jungesellenabschiedsparty*
	stage	*Bühne*
	stairs	*Treppe*
	stamp	*Briefmarke*
	standard of living	*Lebensstandard*
	starter	*Vorspeise*
	station	*Bahnhof*
	stationery	*Schreibwaren*
to	**stay**	*bleiben; wohnen*
	steel	*Stahl*
	steelworks	*Stahlwerk*
to	**step**	*treten*
	stew	*Eintopf*
	stick	*(Holz-)Stock*
to	**stir**	*umrühren*
	stocking	*Strumpf*
	stomach	*Magen*
	stone	*Stein*
	storm	*Gewitter; Sturm*
	stout	*Stout (schwarzes Bier)*
	stranded	*gestrandet*
	strange	*seltsam, merkwürdig*
	stranger	*Fremde(r)*
	strawberry	*Erdbeere*
	street	*Straße*
	strength	*Macht; Stärke*
	strong	*stark*
	stuffing	*Füllung*
	success	*Erfolg*
	successful	*erfolgreich*
	sugar	*Zucker*
	suitable	*passend*
	sunscreen	*Sonnencreme*
	superstition	*Aberglaube*
to	**supply**	*liefern; bereitstellen*
	surface	*Oberfläche*
	surgical	*chirurgisch*
	surname	*Nachname*
to	**surround**	*umgeben*
to	**survive**	*überleben*
	swede	*Steckrübe*

T

	tablespoon	*Esslöffel*
	tabloid	*Boulevardzeitung*
to	**take over**	*übernehmen*
to	**take place**	*stattfinden*
to	**take time**	*(seine) Zeit brauchen*
	tall	*hoch, groß*
	target	*Ziel*
	tart	*Törtchen, Tarte*
	tax	*Steuer*
	tax rate	*Steuersatz*
	taxi rank	*Taxistand*
	tea bag	*Teebeutel*
	teapot	*Teekanne*
	teaspoon	*Teelöffel*
	television	*Fernsehen, Fernseher*
	temporary	*vorübergehend, befristet*
	tennis court	*Tennisplatz*
	Thai	*thailändisch*
	thistle	*Distel*
to	**throw**	*werfen*
	tights	*Strumpfhose*
	tile	*Ziegel*
	time	*Zeit*
	tiny	*winzig*
	toad	*Kröte*
	toad in the hole	*in Teig gebackene Würstchen*
to	**touch**	*anfassen, berühren*
	touch wood	*wenn alles gut geht; toi, toi, toi*
	tournament	*Turnier*
	tower	*Turm*
	town	*Stadt*

trade	*Gewerbe*
traffic lights	*Ampel*
tragedy	*Tragödie*
trainers	*Turnschuhe*
to **translate**	*übersetzen*
treasure	*Schatz*
trip	*Reise, Fahrt*
true	*wahr*
to **try**	*(an)probieren; versuchen*
the Tube	*die (Londoner) U-Bahn*
tubular bells	*Glockenspiel*

U

underground	*U-Bahn*
underprivileged	*benachteiligt*
underwear	*Dessous; Unterwäsche*
unicorn	*Einhorn*
Union Flag	*britische Flagge*
Union Jack	*Union Jack*
United Kingdom	*Vereinigtes Königreich*
unknown	*unbekannt*
unpaid	*nicht bezahlt*
unusual	*außergewöhnlich*
usually	*normalerweise*

V

varied	*unterschiedlich, abwechslungsreich*
variety	*Art; Auswahl*
vegetable	*Gemüse*
venue	*Veranstaltungsort*
Victoria sponge	*mit Sahne und Marmelade gefüllter Biskuitkuchen*
victory	*Sieg*
Viking	*Wikinger(in)*
village	*Dorf*
vintage	*erlesen*
violent	*gewalttätig*
to **visit**	*besuchen; besichtigen*
volunteer	*Ehrenamtliche(r), Freiwillige(r)*

W

waiter	*Kellner*
waitress	*Kellnerin*
to **walk**	*spazieren; zu Fuß gehen*
wall	*Mauer; Wand*
wanderer	*Streuner(in)*
to **warm**	*(auf)wärmen*
to **watch**	*ansehen, beobachten*
to **wear**	*tragen (z. B. Kleidung)*
weather	*Wetter*
wedding	*Hochzeit*
Wellington(s)	*Gummistiefel*
well-known	*bekannt, berühmt*
well-off	*wohlhabend*
wether	*Hammel*
whether	*ob*
white	*weiß*
white pudding	*irische Spezialität: Pastete aus Fleisch und Haferflocken*
wholemeal bread	*Vollkornbrot*
wide	*weit, breit*
wing	*Flügel*
wish	*Wunsch*
wit	*Geist; Wortwitz*
within	*innerhalb*
witty	*geistreich*
work of art	*Kunstwerk*
worm	*Wurm*
to **wrap**	*einpacken*
writer	*Schriftsteller(in), Autor(in)*
writing paper	*Briefpapier*
wrong	*falsch; irrtümlich*

Y

yellow press	*Regenbogenpresse*
Yorkshire pudding	*Yorkshire Pudding*
Your Majesty	*Eure Majestät*
Your Royal Highness	*Eure / Seine / Ihre Königliche Hoheit*
Yours sincerely	*Mit freundlichen Grüßen*

Z

zero	*null*

Bildnachweis

Seite 4: Dartmoor: fotolia.de/ Dual Aspect, Tower Bridge: fotolia.de/ kmiragaya, Orangenmarmelade: fotolia/ Barbara Pheby • **Seite 5 :** Leuchtturm: fotolia.de/ samott, Whisky: fotolia/ Big City Lights, Keltisches Kreuz: istockphoto/ fotoMonkee • **Seite 6/7:** Gummistiefel: fotolia/ Stormcab • **Seite 8:** Karte UK: fotolia/ darknightsky • **Seite 9:** Isambard Kingdom Brunel: fotolia/ Georgios Kollidas, Münzen: fotolia/ Mark A • **Seite 10:** Begrüßung: istockphoto.com/ Neustockimages • **Seite 11:** Flagge England: shutterstock.com/ Lasse Kristensen, Flagge Schottland: shutterstock.com/ Gencay M. Emin, Union Jack: shutterstock/ Lasse Kristensen, Flagge Wales: shutterstock.com/ ruskpp • **Seite 12:** Keltisches Kreuz: istockphoto/ fotoMonkee, Römisches Bad: fotolia/ Patricia Hofmeester, Wikingerschiff: shutterstock/ Algol, Normannische Kirche: fotolia/ AndG, William Shakespeare: Wikimedia Commons • **Seite 13:** Buch „Robinson Crusoe": EKS GmbH, Buch „Lord of the flies": EKS GmbH, Buch „Treasure Island": EKS GmbH, Buch „Gulliver's Travels": EKS GmbH • **Seite 14:** Regenbogen: fotolia/ andreiuc88 • **Seite 16/17:** London: fotolia/ QQ7 • **Seite 19:** Kew Gardens: fotolia/ allyb208, London Eye: fotolia/ slouankang, Houses of Parliament: fotolia/ antonel, St Paul's Cathedral: fotolia/ pauws99 • **Seite 20:** Beefeater: shutterstock/Dennis Debono, Portier: shutterstock/ sculpies, Queen's Guard: shutterstock/ Birute Vijeikiene, Rechtsanwältin: fotolia/ wildworx • **Seite 22:** Drogerieartikel: shutterstock/ Christos Georghiou, Schreibwaren: fotolia/ Dark Vectorangel, Lebensmittel: fotolia/ Piumadaquila, Babyartikel: shutterstock/ glossygirl21 • **Seite 24:** Harrods: shutterstock/ Stuart Monk • **Seite 25:** Tee: fotolia/gtranquillity, Stiefel: fotolia/ Nastasia Froloff, Rolls Royce: shutterstock/ EML, Smartphone: shutterstock/ Umberto Shtanzman • **Seite 26:** Cornish Pasty: shutterstock/ Tobik • **Seite 27:** Küste Devons: fotolia/ acceleratorhams • **Seite 28:** Stonehenge: fotolia/ gianliguori, Tintagel: shutterstock/ stocker1970, Plymouth: fotolia/ samott, Bath: fotolia/ Patricia Hofmeester, Karte: fotolia/ musaffarpatel • **Seite 29:** Glastonbury Tor: fotolia/ Vincent • **Seite 31:** Eden Project: fotolia/ Kevin Jarratt • **Seite 32:** Alice im Wunderland: shutterstock/ Morphart Creation • **Seite 33:** Kokosnusshälften: fotolia/ nanthapa, Diamanten: fotolia/ generation4, Handtuch: fotolia/ Serp, Rotwein und Schokolade: fotolia/ kristina rütten • **Seite 35:** Fliege in Suppe: istock/ Ouchman • **Seite 36:** Lake District: fotolia/ Wallace • **Seite 37:** Manchester: fotolia/ Ant Clausen • **Seite 38:** Karte UK: fotolia/ darknightsky • **Seite 39:** Sting: shutterstock/ Featureflash, Mel C: shutterstock/ Ronen, Ian McKellen: shutterstock/ Featureflash, Judie Dench: shutterstock/ Entertainment Press, Blackpool Tower: fotolia/ lizascotty, York Minster: fotolia/ Pefkos, Angel of the North: fotolia/ drhfoto, Hadrian's Wall: fotolia/ Violetstar • **Seite 41:** Yorkshire Pudding: fotolia/ Joe Gough, Cumberland sausage: fotolia/ Whitebox Media, Eccles cake: shutterstock/ Monkey Business Images, Lancashire hotpot: fotolia/ Monkey Business • **Seite 42:** Königin Victoria: fotolia/ BasPhoto • **Seite 43:** Windsor Castle: fotolia/ Lance Bellers, Balmoral Castle: fotolia/ Louise McGilviray, Buckingham Palace: fotolia/ Renáta Sedmáková, Palace of Westminster: fotolia/ pauws99 • **Seite 44:** Spielkarte König: fotolia/ bobyramone, Spielkarte Königin: fotolia/ bobyramone • **Seite 46/47:** Schottische Highlands: fotolia/ great_photos • **Seite 48:** Karte Schottland: fotolia/ Jürgen Priewe • **Seite 49:** Edinburgh Castle: fotolia/ Andreas Stix, Glasgow Science Centre: fotolia/ David Woods, Whisky-Distillerie: shutterstock/ Jaime Pharr, Ardnamurchan Beach: fotolia/ JAC • **Seite 50:** Haggis: fotolia/ Christelle • **Seite 51:** Whisky: fotolia/ Big City Lights • **Seite 52:** Tennis: fotolia/ Karramba Production, Rugby: fotolia/ Rtimages, Cricket: fotolia/ Brian Jackson, Fußball: fotolia/ Sirena Designs • **Seite 53:** Fußball: fotolia/ Melinda Nagy • **Seite 55:** Badminton: fotolia/ Sergey Tyan, Baseball: fotolia/ Paul Yates, Croquet: fotolia/ Sportactive, Squash: fotolia/ tashka2000, Snooker: fotolia/ Ahileos, Golf: fotolia/ Ray, Boxen: fotolia/ Africa Studio, Darts: fotolia/ Africa Studio • **Seite 56:** Küste: fotolia/ eldo, **Seite 57:** Ortsschild: shutterstock/ Len Green, Küste: fotolia/ eldo • **Seite 59:** Mount Snowdon: fotolia/ Rob Ford, Caernarvon Castle: fotolia/ Gail Johnson, St David's Cathedral: fotolia/ Falk, Tallylyn Railway: fotolia/ DavidYoung • **Seite 60:** Welsh rarebit: fotolia/ Monkey Business • **Seite 61:** Kaninchen: fotolia.de/ Pavel Sazonov, Fenster: shutterstock.com/ Andrey Kekyalyaynen, Glocke: fotolia/ mediagram, Möhren: fotolia.de/Unclesam, Haus: fotolia/ Gail Johnson • **Seite 62:** Schild „Give way": fotolia/ kk_tt, Schild Straße wird schmäler: fotolia/ Sharpshot, Schild „Reduce speed now": fotolia/ Stephen Finn, Schild No parking at any time: shutterstock/ Jostein Hauge, Schild Kreisverkehr: shutterstock/ Eddie J. Rodriquez • **Seite 63:** Doppelte gelbe Linie: fotolia/ Mexrix • **Seite 64:** Bahnhof: fotolia/ Diam • **Seite 65:** Taxi: fotolia/ taxiberlin • **Seite 66:** Kneipenschild: shutter-stock/ Douglas Freer • **Seite 67:** Cream Tea: shutter-stock/ eyedear • **Seite 68:** Victoria sponge: fotolia/ robynmac, Sandwiches: fotolia/ ilolab, Filled Baguette: shutterstock/ Christopher Elwell, Scones: fotolia/ boophotography • **Seite 69:** Teekanne: shutterstock/ Lev Kropotov • **Seite 70:** Chips: fotolia/ Jiri Hera, Brezeln: fotolia/ Harald Biebel, Pork Scratchings: fotolia/ edster1980, Erdnüsse: fotolia/

jeehyun • **Seite 71:** Glas Stout: fotolia/ zaphod2008, Glas Bitter: fotolia/ Neiro-mobile, Glas Lager: shutterstock/ Emin Ozkan • **Seite 72:** Schokolade: fotolia/jeanphilippe delisle, Weetabix: fotolia/ Chris Brignell, Indisches Gericht: fotolia/ Richard Griffin, Kekse: fotolia/ markrussell-photo, Toast mit Marmite: fotolia/ robynmac • **Seite 73:** Bubble and squeak: shutterstock/ Monkey Business Images, Ploughman's Lunch: fotolia/ Monkey Business, Toad in the hole: fotolia/ Joe Gough , Laverbread: istock/ AlasdairJames • **Seite 74:** Sandwiches: shutter-stock/ 3523studio • **Seite 75:** Englisches Frühstück: fotolia.de/ Springfield Gallery • **Seite 76:** Viktoria-nisches Weihnachten: shutterstock/ Victorian Traditions • **Seite 77:** Pfannkuchen: fotolia/ Mihai Simonia • **Seite 78:** Christmas stockings: fotolia/ OlegDoroshin, Hot cross buns: fotolia/ jamierogers1, Kürbislaterne: fotolia/ Africa Studio, Rosen: fotolia/ Africa Studio • **Seite 79:** Mistelzweig: shutterstock/ Krasowit • **Seite 80:** Anstoßen: fotolia.de/ Konstantin Sutyagin • **Seite 81:** Hochzeitstorte: fotolia/ vsurkov, Dosen an Auto: fotolia/ unopix, Zerbrochenes Geschirr: fotolia/ Esther Hildebrandt, Küssendes Paar: shutterstock/ negativkz • **Seite 82:** Houses of Parliament: istock/ oversnap • **Seite 83:** Victory-Zeichen: shutterstock/ Robert Voight • **Seite 85:** Schlagzeile: shutterstock/ justasc, Breaking News: fotolia/ Carsten Reisinger, Wahlurne: Shutterstock/ Andrey Burmakin • **Seite 86:** Stratford-upon-Avon: shutterstock/ David Hughes • **Seite 87:** Ironbridge: fotolia/ Pecold • **Seite 88:** Robin Hood: fotolia/ fotofrank, Shakespeare: shutterstock/ Andrew Roland, Rugby: fotolia/ Rtimages, Therme: shutterstock/ holbox • **Seite 89:** Royal Shakespeare Theatre: fotolia/ david hughes, Warwick Castle: fotolia/ Centaur, Coventry Cathedral: fotolia/ c, Silverstone Rennstrecke: shutterstock/ Michael Stokes • **Seite 90:** Robin Hood: fotolia/ wajan, Pastete: fotolia/ jamierogers1, Würste: fotolia/ Joe Gough, Käse: fotolia/ kristina rütten, Kuchen: fotolia/ Douglas Freer • **Seite 91:** Shakespeare-Buch: istockphoto/ duncan1890 • **Seite 92:** Leinwand: fotolia.de/ Ferenc Szelepcsenyi • **Seite 93:** Sherlock Holmes: shutterstock/ ostill • **Seite 95:** Mos-kauer Kreml: fotolia/ daskleineatelier, Diamanten: fotolia/ generation4, Kalender: fotolia/ sergign, Roulette: fotolia.de/ Irochka • **Seite 96:** Cliffs of Moher: fotolia/ lbs • **Seite 97:** Kleeblatt: fotolia/ arrxxx, Kreuz: fotolia/ Alexey Zarodov • **Seite 99:** Irischer Pass: fotolia/ openyouraperture, Landkarte: shutterstock/ Pontus Edenberg • **Seite 100:** Newgrange: fotolia/ paulflynn, Kinsale: fotolia/ Andrei Nekrassov, Giant's Causeway: fotolia/ luca fabbian, Dublin, Trinity College: fotolia/ Robert Wilson • **Seite 101:** Guiness: fotolia/ zaphod2008 • **Seite 103:** Maske: shutterstock/ Scott Rothstein, Rollschuhe: shutterstock/ Carlos Caetano, Geschmink-tes Kind: fotolia/ Eléonore H, Briefmarke: shutterstock/ Neftali • **Seite 104:** Tate Modern: fotolia/ Alex Yeung, • **Seite 105:** Royal Albert Hall: fotolia/ photomic

Noch nie war Englisch so anschaulich!

Niveau A1 – B2

ISBN: 978-3-12-516080-4
[D] 9,99 € **[A]** 9,99 €

- **Alle Wörter, die Sie brauchen:** 16.000 Wörter und Wendungen aus den wichtigsten Lebensbereichen.
- **Richtig aussprechen:** Mit Lautschrift für jedes englische Wort.
- **Gesehen und einfach gemerkt:** Durch Bilder bleibt der Wortschatz besser haften.
- **Leicht gefunden:** Im zweisprachigen Register schnell das richtige Wort nachschlagen.
- **Plus:** Offline Premium-App.

Sehen, verstehen, gemerkt!
Mit Bildern den gesamten Grund- und Aufbauwortschatz nachschlagen und lernen. Für Anfänger (A1) und Fortgeschrittene (B2).

PONS
www.pons.de